# INTERPRETING
# BEYOND BORDERS

*Fernando F. Segovia*

# THE BIBLE AND POSTCOLONIALISM, 3

Series Editor:
*R.S. Sugirtharajah*

Sheffield
Academic Press

Copyright © 2000 Sheffield Academic Press

Published by
Sheffield Academic Press Ltd
Mansion House
19 Kingfield Road
Sheffield S11 9AS
England


Typeset by Sheffield Academic Press
and
Printed on acid-free paper in Great Britain
by Cromwell Press
Melksham, Wiltshire


British Library Cataloguing in Publication Data

A catalogue record for this book is available
from the British Library


ISBN 1 84127 104 7

# Contents

Part II
**Reading from the Diaspora**

# Acknowledgments

Any volume like this one presupposes the assistance and support of a good number of people, to whom I am deeply indebted and ever thankful. First and foremost, to all those who kindly accepted the invitation to serve as contributors to the project and who wrote out of their own diasporas. Second, to Dr S.R. Sugirtharajah, General Editor of this series on 'The Bible and Postcolonialism', for his most gracious invitation to serve as the editor of the present volume. Third, to Dean Joseph C. Hough Jr, of the Divinity School at Vanderbilt University for his gracious support toward editorial and secretarial expenses. Fourth, to the Revd Yak-Hwee Tan, who, as a doctoral student in New Testament and Christian Origins within the Graduate Department of Religion at Vanderbilt University, served as my editorial assistant for the project, for her superb editing of the project. Fifth, to the entire staff of Sheffield Academic Press, and especially Georgia Litherland and Judith Willson. Finally, to my wife, Dr Elena Olazagasti-Segovia, for sharing, out of her own diaspora, in diaspora with me.

This volume is dedicated to all those critics and theologians from the non-Western world who have come to form part of the diaspora of the Two-Thirds World in the West and who work and struggle, with dignity and tenacity, for liberation and decolonization in and out of their respective diasporas.

# List of Contributors

Marcella María Althaus-Reid
New College, University of Edinburgh, Edinburgh, UK

Francisco García-Treto
Trinity University, San Antonio, Texas, USA

Hemchand Gossai
Culver-Stockton College, Canton, Missouri, USA

Jeffrey Kah-Jin Kuan
Pacific School of Religion, Berkeley, California, USA

Winston Persaud
Wartburg Theological Seminary, Dubuque, Iowa, USA

Fernando F. Segovia
The Divinity School, Vanderbilt University, Nashville, Tennessee, USA

Osvaldo D. Vena
Garrett-Evangelical Theological Seminary, Evanston, Illinois, USA

Sze-kar Wan
Andover-Newton Theological School, Newton Centre, Massachusetts, USA

# Interpreting beyond Borders: Postcolonial Studies and Diasporic Studies in Biblical Criticism

FERNANDO F. SEGOVIA

The juxtaposition of Postcolonial Studies and Diasporic Studies, while perhaps not immediately self-evident, is not difficult to establish. Indeed, these are two fields of studies that are closely interrelated and interdependent. They are also fields of studies that can be and have been brought to bear on Biblical Studies. While the relationship of Postcolonial Studies to biblical criticism continues to be made with increasing force and clarity, that between Diasporic Studies and biblical criticism has not yet received much attention. The essays in this volume on diasporic criticism, or 'interpreting beyond borders', mark a significant step forward in this regard. In the light of such developments, an exploration of the relationship between Postcolonial Studies and Diasporic Studies is very much in order for a proper understanding of their own relationship and application to biblical criticism. This set of relationships I shall pursue here as follows: I begin with an overview of the disciplinary range of Postcolonial Studies, as a way of establishing the place of Diasporic Studies within it; continue with a look at the relationship between Diasporic Studies and biblical criticism from the perspective of Christian Studies; and conclude with an overview of two early diasporic models at work in biblical criticism, as theoretical context for the present project.

## Postcolonial Studies: Disciplinary Range

I take the by now common designation of 'Postcolonial Studies' to signify the study of the realm of the geopolitical—the relationship between center and margins, metropolis and periphery, on a global political scale: the imperial and the colonial. Such a relationship I further see as encompassing both social and cultural 'reality' —social formation and cultural production; consequently, I see the study in question as multidimensional, multiperspectival and multidisciplinary—a task best captured by the use of the plural 'studies', that is, a congeries of studies with a common focus on the geopolitical. This understanding of the field yields, to be sure, a quite extensive vision of its disciplinary range, the parameters of which may be circumscribed from a number of different angles.

To begin with, the adjective (or substantive) 'postcolonial' may be understood in at least two ways, each with its own significant semantic range. At one level, it may be defined in historico-political terms: a reference to that period of time following upon the formal separation or 'independence' of a 'colony' or group of 'colonies' from a governing 'empire'. From this perspective, the term would have wide-ranging application. Taking Western imperialism as the frame of reference, for example, the following divisions would be in order: (1) from the end of the eighteenth century, in the United States of America; (2) through the whole of the nineteenth century, for much of the rest of the Americas, mostly in Latin America but also in the Caribbean; (3) during the course of the twentieth century, for most of Africa, Asia and Oceania, and the Caribbean. At another level, the adjective may be defined along socio-psychological lines: a reference to that frame of mind, individual or collective, that problematizes the imperial/colonial phenomenon as a whole and, in so doing, attains a sense of conscientization. From this perspective, a critical awareness of the imperial/colonial phenomenon—its presuppositions, dynamics, ramifications—can both precede the historico-political process of independence and be absent in newly independent contexts. A 'postcolonial' focus thus covers a temporal (what-follows-the-colonial) as well as a critical application (what-questions-the-colonial).

Second, from the point of view of its historico-political signification, the concept of 'independence' can prove quite ambiguous. In effect, former colonies can attain formal independence but remain or fall under a different sort of domination altogether by their former governing empires or a new configuration of such empires. From this perspective, the 'postcolonial' period of time may never move beyond the formal political phase, since other types of domination and dependence—whether social, economic, cultural or any combination thereof—continue unabated or even intensify. In this scenario the 'postcolonial' simply turns into the 'neocolonial'—a transmogrified version of the imperial/colonial phenomenon. A 'postcolonial' focus is thus concerned with the character of the temporal period in question—the text, the contradictions, the subtext.

Third, from the point of view of its psycho-sociological signification, the notion of 'conscientization' immediately brings to the fore the issue of opposition or resistance to the imperial/colonial phenomenon. As such, a postcolonial focus encompasses not only the discourses of imposition and domination but also the anti-discourses of opposition and resistance.

Fourth, the adjective (or substantive) 'postcolonial' is a compound term: a juxtaposition of the Latin temporal preposition *post* as prefix and the adjective 'colonial' as stem (derived from the Latin *colonia*, meaning 'farm' or 'settlement'). I make such an obvious point only to underscore the fact that the term 'colonial' may be used by itself or in combination with a number of prefixes— such as 'pre', 'post', 'neo'—to indicate phases within colonialism itself. The postcolonial focus covers all of these different stages.

Lastly, it should be clear from all of the above that the term 'colonial', in any of its variations, presupposes and points to the presence of the term 'imperial', which, as a result, can be used as well either by itself or in combination with the very same prefixes ('pre'; 'post'; 'neo') to indicate corresponding phases within imperialism itself. In other words, a colonial formation of any sort always implies and entails an imperial formation of the same sort. The 'postcolonial' focus covers as well all of these different phases or stages within imperialism.

In the light of these observations, the disciplinary range of 'Postcolonial Studies' can be represented as follows:

—The study of imperialism and colonialism, which I understand as follows: while the former focuses on all that pertains to the center or metropolis, the latter marks all that pertains to the margins or periphery.

—The study of imposition and domination as well as of opposition and resistance: not only the discourses of imperialism and colonialism but also the counterdiscourses of anti-imperialism and anti-colonialism.

—The study of the different phases or periods within imperialism and colonialism, with their resultant subdiscourses: pre-imperialism and pre-colonialism; imperialism and colonialism; post-imperialism and post-colonialism; neo-imperialism and neo-colonialism.

The result is a remarkably extensive disciplinary range.[1] To complicate matters even further, I would add that the phenomenon of the diaspora can be studied both as a discourse in its own right, as Diasporic Studies, and as a subdiscourse within the discursive framework of Postcolonial Studies. Thus, I would argue that, at the core of the imperial/colonial phenomenon, indeed through all of its various stages, lies the reality and experience of the diasporic phenomenon: un-settlement, travel, re-settlement. Consequently, it should come as no surprise that the application of Diasporic Studies to biblical criticism should follow not long after that of Postcolonial Studies. Once the discourse of the postcolonial began to be deployed in biblical criticism, it was only a matter of time before the subdiscourse of the diasporic would be invoked as well, especially in the light of drastic changes at work within criticism itself.

## Diasporic Studies and Biblical Criticism

Given such connections and developments, I turn to examine in greater detail the relationship between Diasporic Studies and biblical criticism within the overall conjunction of Postcolonial Stud-

1.    Such a range, I have argued (Segovia 1999), proves highly problematic. On the one hand, I regard the use of 'Postcolonial Studies' to designate such a massive field of studies quite appropriate. Thus, relying upon the psycho-sociological understanding of 'postcolonial', one can readily argue that the whole of the imperial/colonial phenomenon comes under critical scrutiny. On the other hand, I view such use as misleading as well. In effect, the whole phenomenon is being described in terms of one of its parts, thus making for a classic and confusing study of synecdoche. For such reasons I much prefer a different and more comprehensive designation for this field of studies, such as Imperial/Colonial Studies. Quite aside from the issue of nomenclature, the point is that the field of studies in question is quite extensive, not only in terms of approaches but also in terms of content.

ies and biblical criticism. I begin with a word about diaspora and Diasporic Studies in general—the character and parameters of the field in its own right. From there I go on to examine the relevance of the diasporic phenomenon and Diasporic Studies for biblical criticism. In so doing, my primary focus shall be on criticism within the Christian tradition, for reasons that have to do with the changing nature of this tradition and that shall become evident in the course of the ensuing discussion. While the relevance of Diasporic Studies for criticism in the Jewish tradition is obvious, given the long-standing and wide-ranging experience of diaspora within Judaism, such a focus lies beyond the concerns and goal of the present study, although I shall make use of such criticism in the final section.

*Diaspora and Diasporic Studies*
The term 'diaspora'—borrowed directly from the Greek (*diaspora*), where it means 'scattering' or 'dispersion' (cf. *diaspeirō*, 'to scatter' or 'to spread about')[2]— ranges in signification from the more concrete to the more general, yielding in turn definitions along maximalist or minimalist lines. This difference in signification also proves largely sequential in nature, with a shift away from a highly essentialist to a highly functionalist type of definition.

Traditionally, the term has been applied to the exile of the Jews away from their historical homeland and among countless other lands and peoples. This identification has been so consistent and so powerful that William Safran, a student of the diasporic phenomenon (1991: 83-84), has classified the Jewish diaspora as the 'ideal type' for all diasporas, with all other examples of the phenomenon—and he does allow for other examples, provided that they meet the criteria of the essentialist definition invoked—characterized as 'metaphorical designations' (p. 83), of which none, he adds, 'fully conforms' (p. 84) to the ideal type. Safran's ideal-type definition is of a maximalist sort, consisting of a core affirmation ('expatriate minority communities') and an extended set of characteristics that members of such communities must hold in common.

---

2. The term itself is compound, consisting of the preposition *dia* (in different directions) as prefix and the substantive *spora* (sowing) as stem (cf. *speirō* , 'to sow').

These characteristics, six in all, are identified as follows: (1) Dispersal, either of themselves or of their ancestors, from a specific original 'center' to two or more 'peripheral' or foreign regions. (2) Retention of a collective memory, vision or myth about the original homeland—its physical location, history and achievements. (3) Belief that they are not and perhaps cannot be fully accepted by the host society, leading to feelings of partial alienation and insulation from it. (4) View of ancestral homeland as true, ideal home and the place to which they or their descendants would or should eventually return, given appropriate conditions. (5) Belief in collective commitment to the maintenance or restoration of original homeland, its safety and prosperity. (6) Continued relation, personally or vicariously, to the ancestral homeland in some way, with ethnocommunal consciousness and solidarity as importantly defined by the existence of such a relationship. At the same time, not all characteristics need be present, only an unspecified 'several', and no one characteristic in particular is regarded as indispensable.

More recently, within the ambit of Cultural Studies, the term has taken on much broader signification. The following definitions, taken from cultural dictionaries, provide representative examples of such expansion of meaning: for Radhika Subramanian (1966), the term covers 'a range of territorial displacements, either forced, as indenture or slavery, or voluntary emigration'; for Ashcroft, Griffiths and Tiffin (1998), diasporas emerge as 'the voluntary or forcible movements of peoples from their homelands into new regions'. Such geographical definitions are of a minimalist sort, involving a core affirmation (territorial displacement or movement away from homeland into other regions) and a brief additional qualification to the effect that such translation may be voluntary or coerced.[3] Such definitions also resemble very closely the kind of definition specifically challenged by Safran, which he associates in particular with the work of Walker Connor (1986: 16), for whom

3.    The two core affirmations are not at all dissimilar: what Safran means by 'expatriate communities' is, I believe, precisely this notion of 'territorial displacement' or 'movements away from homeland into other regions'. What Safran does add is the observation that such communities are also 'minority communities', a feature that, I also believe, would not be disputed by the broader definitions, though it is not made explicit.

diaspora simply becomes 'that segment of a people living outside the homeland'. For Safran (1991: 83) such functionalist definitions prove far too general in application: insofar as they encompass such categories of people as 'expatriates, expellees, political refugees, alien residents, immigrants, and ethnic and racial minorities *tout court*', they end up rendering the term meaningless, utterly devoid of content.

Given my own view of meaning as construction, ever pliant and ever shifting, I much prefer a minimalist approach, with its emphasis on geographical dispersion or scattering from one's own land and people to somebody else's land and people.[4] Such a functionalist type of definition, I find, has much to recommend itself. To begin with, it does away with defining criteria whose source is never quite clear: the characteristics in question are simply enumerated and taken as normative. While the logic of the argument would seem to point toward the derivation of such criteria from the Jewish experience of diaspora, such a move is never explained or justified. In addition, it dispenses with any need for an ideal-type diaspora in the light of which all pretenders, so to speak, would be examined and evaluated. The attempt to turn a particular experience of diaspora into an ideal-type construct I find highly problematic. Finally, it focuses on the common denominator of the diaspora experience: geographical translation. In so doing, it allows for a wide number of applications and hence for the possibility of extensive and illuminating comparative exercises across time and culture.

From this perspective, therefore, Diasporic Studies would be concerned with the analysis of geographical translations of peoples in general, whether in the present or in the past, whether in the West or outside the West. Such breadth of application, I would argue, should be seen not as rendering the term devoid of content, a meaningless signifier, but rather as charging it with an abundance of content, a multifarious signifier. In other words, the common geographical denominator—what I have referred to above as

4.   Interestingly enough, however, I should point out that my own diaspora, from Cuba to the United States, qualifies as a legitimate use of the term according to Safran's definition, along with such other diasporas as the Armenian, Maghrebi, Turkish, Palestinian, Greek and Chinese at present and the Polish in the past (1991: 84, 90).

the phenomenon of un-settlement, travel, re-settlement—admits of countless variations, which allow in turn for countless exercises in comparison.

*Relevance of Diaspora and Diasporic Studies*
Such a maximalist definition of the diasporic phenomenon and comprehensive view of Diasporic Studies have immediate and profound relevance for the practice of biblical criticism in the contemporary world. This relevance I shall trace in terms of Postcolonial Studies, Christianity and Christian Studies.

*Postcolonial Studies*. From the point of view of Postcolonial Studies, as already indicated, diasporas form part and parcel of the entire imperial/colonial phenomenon, insofar as the latter entails, from the very beginning and at every step of the way, the geographical translation of peoples, coerced or voluntary, from homelands to other lands. Taking Western imperialism and colonialism as frame of reference, at least three major phases in geographical translation can be readily outlined:

First, the process of colonization that paralleled the development of Western imperialism involved a massive dispersion of Europeans throughout the entire world. Untold millions proceeded to settle everywhere and in so doing established countless 'neo-Europes'—as Alfred Crosby has aptly termed such communities—outside of Europe. Indeed, Crosby (1986) estimates that between 1820 and 1930 alone the ranks of people leaving the European subcontinent numbered around fifty million. The resultant web of diasporas and settlements had enormous consequences for non-Western peoples across the entire spectrum—from the social to the cultural, from the economic to the political, from the religious to the educational, and so forth—of their respective societies.

Second, this process of colonization engendered, in turn, a massive dispersion of non-Western peoples from their historical homelands. Once again, untold millions were settled, mostly by way of slavery and indenture, in other areas of the colonial world as sources of cheap labor for the system of production of early capitalism. The resultant web of diasporas and settlements had enormous consequences as well across the globe, not only in the historical homelands left behind but also in the new lands in question, where highly mixed societies and peoples eventually came to be, especially in the 'new world'.

Third, in more recent times this process of colonization has further engendered a new and massive dispersion of non-Western peoples from their own homelands, whether historical or imposed. Yet again, untold millions have begun to settle, by way of legal and illegal migration, in the West, given the economic forces at work in the system of production of late capitalism. There should be little doubt that the ramifications of such a web of diasporas and settlements will prove, in time, just as enormous for the West, across the entire spectrum of its respective societies.

In the end, therefore, the process of geographical translation at the heart of the Western imperial/colonial phenomenon may be said to have come full circle: what began in the late fifteenth century with dispersion from Europe outward, leading to a massive European diaspora of global proportions, has yielded in the late twentieth century to dispersion from outside the West into the West, leading to a massive non-Western diaspora of global proportions within the West itself, above all in North America (Canada and the United States) but also in Europe. Thus, just as the West succeeded in establishing itself quite prominently in the non-West over the greater part of the last five hundred years, so has the non-West begun to establish itself quite firmly in the West in the course of the last few decades.

*Christianity.* The consequences for religion in general and for the Christian religion in particular of this process of geographical translation set in motion by the Western imperial/colonial phenomenon have proved fundamental. Over the last five centuries, but above all in the course of the twentieth century, Western expansionism brought about the globalization of Christianity. The result was a twofold impact: that of Christianity on the non-Western religions encountered in the colonial world and that of the colonial world on Christianity as the religion of the West. Just as Christianity deeply affected the religions that it came across during the process of colonization, so has Christianity itself been profoundly touched by its own experience outside the West. In the end, therefore, this process of globalization—driven throughout by the desire to transform 'the other' and thus undertaken with a

spirit of mission and conversion, of exclusivism and superiority—
has yielded self-transformation at the hands of such others as well.

In this regard I find the thesis of Andrew Walls (Professor Emer-
itus of the Study of Christianity in the Non-Western World at the
University of Edinburgh), regarding the historical development of
Christianity quite to the point (1995). Walls speaks of three major
shifts in Christianity's center of gravity, all of which have entailed
not only major geographical and demographic changes but also
substantial cultural and religious changes, as Christianity mutates,
in recurring cycles of recession and expansion, from an already
existing theater of operations to an altogether new one. It is the
third of these shifts that I find most relevant. In this third mutation, identified with the last five hundred years of Western expansionism and paved for by accompanying missionary movements
throughout, Christianity has turned from territorial Christendom
to global Christianity—away from its Western base, where it under-
goes decline in the face of the forces of modernity, toward the non-
Western world, where it witnesses incredible growth.[5] The result is
what Walls calls the non-Western formation of Christianity.

Although five hundred years in the making, as Walls points out,
it is really in the course of the last century that this mutation becomes evident. At the heart of this transformation, still very much
ongoing, lies the phenomenon of globalization: the drastic change
in the demographics of Christian communities across the entire
ecclesiastical spectrum brought about by deliberate, intensive and
highly successful worldwide expansion. If the century began in the
throes of a crusade to make 'the Christian century' a reality by

5.    The first two shifts are described as follows: (a) in the first mutation—
firmly in place by the fourth century and paved for by a mission to the Gentiles that goes back to the first century—Christianity turns from a demographically Jewish phenomenon, centered in Jewish Palestine and culturally
defined by Judaism, to a demographically and culturally Hellenistic-Roman
phenomenon, dispersed across the Mediterranean and the Roman Empire;
(b) in the second mutation—tied to the collapse of the Roman Empire in
both its eastern (in the face of Islam) and western (at the hands of the bar-
barians) provinces and anticipated by the mission outside the imperial frontiers—Christianity turns from the urban centers of the Mediterranean to a new
setting among the Celtic and Germanic peoples between the Atlantic and the
Carpathians and thus among cultivators and semi-settled raiders, where it acquires its territorial sense of 'Christendom'.

spreading the Christian religion to all corners of the world, it ends with such a reality very much in place, from Africa to Asia and the Pacific to Latin America and the Caribbean. The numerical figures in question—heightened as they are by the highly distinctive demographic development of this century, with population explosion in the non-Western world and population stabilization (even decline) in the West—are simply astounding. The following statistics, fragile as they may be, drive the point home in no uncertain fashion (Barrett 1982: 1-20):

a. While in 1900 approximately 65 per cent of the world's Christians lived in Europe or North America, today that figure is estimated to be about 35 per cent. Similarly, while in 1900 Christians in Africa, Asia and Oceania, Latin America and the Caribbean represented 17.2 per cent of global Christianity, today that figure is placed at 60.3 per cent.

b. In the course of the past one hundred years, the following changes in percentage with respect to the number of Christians worldwide are noted: in Africa, from 1.8 per cent to 19.5 per cent; in Asia and Oceania, from 4.3 per cent to 12.5 per cent; in Latin America and the Caribbean, from 11.1 per cent to 28.3 per cent.

Such figures could be endlessly multiplied, but the point is clear: what Walls has characterized as the non-Western formation of the Christian religion is already very much upon us and still very much on the rise. A further and critical twist to this development cannot be ignored. This non-Western formation of Christianity is to be found not only outside the West but also, and increasingly so, within the West itself. The reason is none other than the above-noted radical shift in global patterns of migration: since mid-century, and above all in the last two to three decades, the earlier flow of population from Europe to the rest of the world, including North America, has experienced a sharp reverse, with large-scale immigration now flowing from the whole of the non-Western world into the West—Europe, to be sure, but above all anglophone North America (Canada and the United States).

The United States, for example, is presently undergoing as profound an ethnic transformation as that which took place from 1880 through 1920. Just as that earlier wave of immigration—composed of southern and eastern Europeans and involving Catholic Christians, Jews and Orthodox Christians—changed the face and tenor of the country forever, so will the present wave—composed of immigrants from Africa, Asia and the Pacific, Latin America and the Caribbean—change forever as well the visage and discourse of the country. The statistics are, once again, most telling (US Census Bureau 1995):

a. While in 1980 the non-Hispanic white population numbered 80.0 per cent, in 1995 that percentage had decreased to 73.6 per cent. The projections call for this segment of the population to decrease to 60.5 per cent in 2030 and 52.8 per cent in 2050.

b. Between 1980 and 1995, the major minority groups experienced the following increase in population: Asians, from 1.5 per cent to 3.3 per cent; Africans, from 11.5 per cent to 12.0 per cent; Hispanic, from 6.4 per cent to 10.5 per cent. The projections for 2030 and 2050 run, respectively, as follows: Asians, 6.6 per cent and 8.2 per cent; Africans, 13.1 per cent and 13.6 per cent; Hispanics, 18.9 per cent and 24.5 per cent.

While non-Western immigration into Europe is largely non-Christian in character, such immigration into the United States does have a strong Christian component, as it is becoming quite evident in Christian churches around the country, across the entire ecclesiastical spectrum. Given the demographic projections, moreover, it is clear that Christianity in the United States, at the very core of the contemporary West, will become increasingly 'global', less Western and more non-Western in origins and composition.

*Christian Studies.* Such demographic developments have already brought massive and fundamental changes in the character and shape of Christianity. Such changes have inevitably and radically begun to affect the practices and beliefs of Christianity at all levels, from the manifold venues of everyday life among believers to the defining and ruling centers of institutional life to the learned and knowledge-producing circles of academic life. This is a shift, moreover, that, for all practical purposes, has only just begun. What its ultimate effects will be for global Christianity both outside the West and in the West will not be fully grasped until a century or two from now. It does seem safe to say, however, that the past dominance of the West in the formulation and direction of Christianity will gradually but inexorably yield to a much more decentered and diversified formation. In the process, all beliefs and practices in

the everyday life of believers, all matters of definition and gover-
nance in the institutional life of the churches, and all disciplines
in the academic study of the Christian religion will be directly and
fundamentally affected.

Indeed, the whole of Christian Studies has already been affected
and will continue to be affected as a result of such globalization.
In the process the relevance of Postcolonial Studies and Diasporic
Studies becomes increasingly evident. In the light of the worldwide expansion and demographic transformation of Christianity
brought about by the Western imperial/colonial phenomenon,
Postcolonial Studies can be brought to bear on every aspect of
Christian Studies. Similarly, in the light of the diasporic phenomena involved in such expansion and transformation, above all the
increasing presence of non-Western Christians in the West, Diasporic Studies can also be brought to bear on every aspect of Christian Studies.

Biblical criticism, I would argue, is no exception. Indeed, as
Christianity becomes more and more global, as more and more
non-Western Christians continue to find their way into the West,
and as more and more non-Western Christians continue to enter
the ranks of the discipline within the West itself, the angle of vision
afforded by such a web of diasporic experiences will be increasingly applied to what I regard as the different dimensions constitutive of the discipline at this point in its history:

a. At the level of the ancient texts, where both the Hebrew Scriptures and the Christian Scriptures reveal the experience of diaspora (un-settlement, travel, re-settlement) and where the Christian
Scriptures point to a Christianity in worldwide expansion as well—
all in the context of varying imperial/colonial formations.

b. At the level of modernist readings and readers of these texts,
insofar as the rise and development of the discipline parallel the
climax of Western expansionism and diaspora from the early nineteenth century through the third quarter of the twentieth century
—all in the context of varying imperial/colonial formations.

c. At the level of postmodernist readings and readers of these
texts, as the discipline begins to be directly affected, in the last
quarter of the twentieth century, by the entry of non-Westerners
both outside the West and in diaspora within the West—all in the
context of varying imperial/colonial formations.

## Diasporic Criticism: Early Models

I stated in the introduction that the relationship between Diasporic Studies and biblical criticism had, unlike that between Postcolonial Studies and biblical criticism, not yet received much attention. Yet some initial work has already been done along these lines, so that the exercises contained in this volume, as they themselves generally concede, do not stand in a theoretical vacuum. I bring these reflections on 'interpreting beyond borders' to a close, therefore, with a comparative overview of two attempts to bring diasporic experience and biblical interpretation into dialogue with one another: the first comes from the Jewish diaspora—Daniel Boyarin's analysis of the politics of identity in Paul of Tarsus; the second, from the non-Western Christian diaspora—my own construction of a hermeneutics of the diaspora.

Given my emphasis on the Christian tradition, the inclusion of Boyarin might seem, at first glance, surprising, if not altogether out of place. A word of explanation is in order. As anticipated above, such emphasis on my part was meant to highlight a particular angle of vision within the discipline not only already at work but also bound to expand significantly in the years to come, given the geographical and migratory patterns in both the world at large and Christianity in particular. Needless to say, any explicit reflection on or from the diaspora out of the Jewish tradition must certainly be taken into consideration as well. That of Boyarin I find especially significant in three respects: first, because of his extended dialogue with Paul, a key figure in the discourse of Christianity; second, because of the focus of such dialogue, the politics of identity; and third, because of his view of such dialogue as having contemporary repercussions, not only for Jews and Christians but also but also for West and non-West alike.

*Paul from the Jewish Diaspora*[6]
For Boyarin Paul of Tarsus presents a profound challenge to Jewish notions of identity (1994: 228-29). As such, he argues, Paul's letters

---

6.  I rely primarily on Boyarin's volume on Paul (1994), especially the first chapter ('Circumcision, Allegory, and Universal "Man"') and last chapter ('Answering the Mail: Toward a Radical Jewishness'). The argument is well summarized in an article jointly authored with Jonathan Boyarin (1993).

address all Jews, whether in the past or in the present, and demand a response in return; such a response he offers as a '(post)modern Jew' (p. 228). As point of departure for his analysis of Paul's challenge and his response from the diaspora, I find his three-stage history of Israel quite useful (pp. 257-58). The first stage presents a people or 'tribe' very similar in certain respects to other 'tribes' or peoples in similar material conditions around the world, with a view of itself as unique, as the People, and of its land as singular, as the Land. Such a description, Boyarin immediately adds, is very much of an oversimplification, since this people never actually lived alone or saw itself as autochthonous in the land.[7] The second stage finds this people in cultural, social and political contact with other peoples, making their previous form of life increasingly untenable, both politically and morally. For Boyarin this stage coincides with the Hellenistic period, which comes to a climax with the crises of the first century. The third stage is constituted by diasporic existence, understood not as the inevitable outcome of war but as a voluntary choice, already in practice for centuries prior to the destruction of Judaea. Boyarin sees the way of diaspora as the specific rabbinic answer to the crises: renunciation of domination over others through perpetual renunciation of power.

It is within such diasporic existence, 'invented' by the rabbis in the land (p. 258), that Boyarin constructs his own identity as Jew and from which he offers his critique of Paul as well as of Zionism. Such an exercise entails a look backward, a historical analysis of the world of first-century Judaism, and a look outwards, an ideological analysis of the world of contemporary Judaism.

7. Boyarin foregrounds (pp. 251-53) the complexity of the Jewish discourse of the land, a discourse with two diametrically opposed moments. On the one hand, it is a discourse very similar to that of many 'indigenous' peoples of the world: there is a sense of rootedness in the land. On the other hand, it is a discourse not of autochthony but of always coming from somewhere else. The distinction between 'indigenous' and 'autochthonous' is important: the former is a political claim (people who belong here, who have a rightful claim to the land); the latter, a mystified claim (people who were never anywhere else but here, who have a natural right to the land). The result is a discourse of the land with a self-critique: the sense of a natural, organic connection with the land, a settlement in the land, is accompanied by a sense of perpetual unsettlement. Such self-critique, Boyarin adds, is applicable to all discourses of identity based on autochthony.

*Historical Framework.* For Boyarin the crises of first-century Judaism provoke a variety of responses regarding the question of identity. He focuses on two in particular, which he develops along the lines of a binomial opposition: Christianity, via Paul, which stands for spirit and universalism; Judaism, via the rabbis, which stands for body and particularism (pp. 232-36). Both responses are portrayed as conflicted, generating their own forms of racism as well as of antiracism. Given its emphasis on universality, the 'genius' of Christianity lies in its concern for all peoples; such concern, however, can easily turn into coercion. When combined with power, universalism tends toward imperialism, cultural annihilation, even genocide. Given its emphasis on particularity, the 'genius' of Judaism lies in its ability to leave other people alone; such ability, however, can easily turn into neglect of others. When combined with power, particularism tends toward tribal warfare or fascism.

At the root of the universalist pole lies Paul, whom Boyarin describes as a radical Jew and situates within a specific intellectual tradition in Hellenistic thought (pp. 22-25, 229-32). The key to Paul's response, and to the reading of the corpus, is identified with the baptismal formula taken over by Paul in Gal. 3.26-29: baptism into Christ means putting on Christ, whereby all become one in Christ, so that there is no longer Jew or Greek, slave or freeman, male or female. Thus, driven to find a place for the Gentiles in the Torah, Paul advances a vision of human unity and solidarity based on a combination of Hebrew monotheism and Greek (middle Platonic) universals. This vision Boyarin regards as brilliant but dangerous, insofar as the same signifier, 'Jew', comes to stand for both universalism and discord.

The universalist dimension is evident. With baptism into Christ, a new birth takes place whereby a literal genealogy is substituted by an allegorical one: all bodily differences, including those between Jews and Gentiles, disappear, since the Spirit recognizes no such marks. With this replacement of the corporeal body of the individual by the allegorical body of Christ, those in Christ participate in the allegorical meaning of the promise to Abraham and his seed. For Paul such universal sameness represented the fulfillment of Judaism, now defined not in terms of descent or practice according to the flesh but rather of entry into the body of

Christ. Anyone could be Jewish, therefore, and those who call themselves Jews need not be Jewish at all. The discordant dimension is just as clear. Within this discourse of sameness, bodily difference, such as that represented by Jewish ethnic and cultural specificity, becomes a site of disorder and a focus of coercion. With Paul, therefore, the seeds of anti-Judaism and anti-Semitism are sown, 'almost against his will' (p. 229) in Christian discourse; indeed, as paganism recedes from view, real Jews become the symbol of oppositional difference.

At the root of the particularist pole stand the rabbis, whom Boyarin also places within a particular intellectual strand in Jewish tradition (pp. 36-38, 234-36, 251-56). Against any split of body and spirit and any sort of allegorical genealogy, the rabbis insist on the centrality of peoplehood, the ethnic and cultural specificity of Judaism. Following the nomadic tradition and the Mosaic covenant of antiroyalism rather than the territorial tradition and the Davidic covenant of royalism, such particularism was focused on the body rather than on the land. Indeed, from within a context of diaspora in their own land, the rabbis renounced the land until the final redemption and focused instead on memory of the land. They did so because they saw possession of the land as the greatest threat to continued Jewish cultural practice and difference. Faced, therefore, with a choice between ethnocentricity without domination over others and political domination with loss of specificity, the rabbis opted for the former and, in so doing, advanced the vision of diaspora existence, with its emphasis on bodily identification. This vision Boyarin regards as appropriate but problematic, though much more benign as well.

Rabbinic Judaism never produced the sort of violence engendered by universalist Christianity: its rejection of others did not go beyond such minor practices as spitting on the synagogue floor or avoiding the passing of pagan or Christian places of worship. However, driven by its determined resistance to assimilation and annihilation in the diaspora, rabbinic Judaism did produce a praxis of communal charity (education; feeding; providing for the sick; caring for prisoners) that was not extended unto others. Thus, diasporic Judaism, while not seeking to Judaize the other, did remain content to devote its resources to itself rather than to humanity at large. While such praxis constitutes a quite appropriate ethical stance for an embattled minority, it becomes quite problematic in a situation of political power or growing interdependence.

*Ideological Framework.* In the light of a Judaism that has attained political power and of a world that has become increasingly inter-dependent, Boyarin proposes a resolution of this binomial oppos-ition along the lines of a Hegelian synthesis (pp. 236-46, 256-59). This resolution remains firmly rooted in the diasporic vision of rabbinic Judaism, while incorporating the universalist vision of Pauline Christianity. The result is a vision of diaspora that brings together: (1) the particularism of the body preserved by the rab-bis, with its insistence on the centrality of peoplehood and Jewish ethnic and cultural difference, against the universalism of the spirit envisioned by Paul, with its insistence on unity and sameness in Christ; and (2) the concern for all peoples of the world, present in Pauline Christianity, against the neglect of others in favor of the family, at work in rabbinic Judaism. For Boyarin such a vision is more than an utopian dream, given its grounding in historical ex-perience. It is a vision of 'idealized' diaspora, involving a general-ization of those elements that have marked the best of times for diasporic Judaism: relative freedom from persecution, allowing for full participation in the common cultural life of the contexts in question and even the espousal of radical causes for human liber-ation, while hanging on to ethnic and cultural specificity.

This way of idealized diaspora Boyarin offers as an alternative model to that of national self-determination, characterized as a Western imposition on the world. Such a model presupposes a notion of identity in which there are 'only slaves but no masters' (pp. 248-49), marked by a respect for cultural differences and an encouragement of mutual interaction. Such identity holds that cul-tures endure not by protection from mixing but as a result of such mixing, so that cultures are always in process. Idealized diasporic identity emerges, therefore, as a 'disaggregated' identity (p. 243), allowing, for example, for partially Jewish and partially Greek bod-ies. Idealized diaspora thus stands in opposition to any concept of an essential Jewish culture or any notion of a natural and organic connection between a land and a people. To the contrary, it holds that there can be devotion to a cultural tradition alongside interaction with other traditions and that there can be a people without a land.

In the end, Boyarin's proposal leads to a critique of contemporary Judaism. Indeed, idealized diaspora is proposed as an alternative to Zionism, characterized as a nationalist creation along Western lines (pp. 247-51, 255-60). While acceptable as an 'emergency and temporary rescue operation' (p. 249), the Zionist solution is portrayed as a subversion rather than the culmination of Jewish culture, given its deviation from the traditional rabbinic way of repudiation of power or, at best, sharing of power with others. Its results, given its combination of ethnocentrism and hegemony, have proved disastrous for Israel's others, the Palestinians. Idealized diaspora envisions, therefore, a very different sort of Israel: complete separation of religion and state; revocation of the Law of Return and all cultural, discursive practices that code the state as a Jewish state; equality for all of its citizens and collectivities. In sum, a multinational and multicultural Israel.

Boyarin's (post)modern response to Paul's challenge is clear. In opposition to the universalism inherent in Western discourse, grounded in Paul, with its twofold discourse of sameness and coercion, idealized diaspora offers a combination of particularism and renunciation of power, grounded in the rabbis, alongside a vision of universal human solidarity grounded in Paul. In so doing, Boyarin modifies the vision of diasporic existence 'invented' by the rabbis. The result is a practical vision intended not only for contemporary Judaism but also for the world at large. Indeed, for Boyarin the diasporic option may well represent the best contribution Judaism can make to the contemporary world, given its resistance to any type of universalization as well as its dissociation of ethnicity and hegemony.

*Hermeneutics from the Non-Western Christian Diaspora*
For the last few years I have been engaged in the conceptualization and articulation of a critical stance and program grounded in my own experience and reality of the diaspora. This diaspora is one of exile: born and socialized in Latin America, in the Republic of Cuba within the context of the Caribbean, my family emigrated for sociopolitical reasons to the United States of America in the early 1960s. This diaspora also reveals two major and inter-

related components. On the one hand, as both date and rationale indicate, it was directly tied to the sustained ideological confrontation between West and East—between the 'First World' of capitalist democracy and the 'Second World' of central planning communism—from the end of World War II to the end of the Cold War (1945–89). On the other hand, as the points of departure and destination reveal, it was also an early example of the massive dispersion of the non-Western world in the West—of the 'Third World' of the 'developing' countries in the 'First World' of the 'developed' countries—about to explode in the decades to follow.

In effect, long a neocolonial dependency of the United States, Cuba had become, upon the success of the Revolution in 1959 and its eventual Marxist–Leninist turn in 1961, a neocolonial dependency of the Soviet Union. My family, which had fought for the Revolution against the corrupt and tyrannical government of Fulgencio Batista y Zaldívar, found itself in time opposing the new political turn of events and ultimately going into an exile that can only be described as at once voluntary and coerced. For me the result was a second socialization at the heart of the developed and colonizing West and a sense of being in two places and no place at the one and same time. It was out of this sense, internal as well as external, of both belonging and otherness in Latin America and the United States that I sought to construct a hermeneutics of the diaspora. The following points stand as central to such a program and stance in biblical criticism thus far.

First, I posited a highly contested disciplinary context within Biblical Studies involving a variety of competing paradigms—historical, literary, sociocultural, and ideological (Segovia 1995a). I further argued that the most recent of these, cultural studies, brings fully to the fore the construct of the real reader: the flesh-and-blood reader, always positioned (the question of social location) and interested (the question of social agenda) (Segovia 1995c). This paradigm looks upon all recreations of textual meaning and all reconstructions of ancient history as well as upon all methods and models employed in such recreations and reconstructions as constructions on the part of positioned and interested real readers. Consequently, the paradigm demands a joint critical study of texts and readers and calls for a distinctly ideological mode of discourse in so doing.

Second, I pointed to diversity as a fundamental consequence of Cultural Studies in biblical criticism. Such diversity is evident in two respects. First, with respect to readers, since the model regards and analyzes all readers as positioned and interested, yielding in the process a broad array of reader-constructs or -positions in terms of locations and agendas. Second, with regard to texts, since cultural studies posits behind all texts and histories, all methods and models, real readers, yielding thereby an equally broad variety of reading-constructs or -results in terms of 'texts' and 'histories' as well as strategies and frameworks. The result is a mode of discourse that is not only profoundly ideological but also profoundly polyglot in character, given the highly complex situation of multiple reader-constructs and reading-constructs in question.

Third, within this highly ideological and polyglot critical formation, I advanced a theoretical framework and reading strategy of my own. With regard to model, what I have come to call a hermeneutics of otherness and engagement, I opted for a view of texts, readings of texts (reading-constructs or 'texts'), and readers of texts (reader-constructs) as others—not 'others' to be bypassed, overwhelmed and manipulated but others to be acknowledged, respected and engaged (Segovia 1995b). With regard to strategy, what I have come to describe as intercultural criticism, I adopted an approach to texts, readings of texts and readers of texts as literary or aesthetic, rhetorical or strategic, and ideological or political products—not only to be analyzed as others but also to be engaged in critical dialogue (Segovia 1995d).

Finally, I further linked strategy and framework to the problematic of postcolonial studies, with their geopolitical focus on the crosscultural and transhistorical phenomenon of imperial and colonial formations (Segovia 1998). Such a geopolitical optic I see as directly applicable to the various constitutive dimensions of biblical criticism foregrounded in Cultural Studies: (1) the world of 'antiquity'—the world of texts, given their origins in a variety of imperial formations, with specific emphasis on the Roman Empire as the setting for early Christianity; (2) the world of 'modernity'—the world of readers and readings of traditional biblical criticism, given its rise and development in the West, on both sides of the North Atlantic, during the climactic period of Western imperial formations in the nineteenth and early twentieth centuries; (3) the world of 'postmodernity'—the world of readers and readings of contemporary biblical criticism, given its appearance and proliferation in the non-Western world as well as among non-Western minorities in the Western world.

*Concluding Comments*

These two early models of diasporic criticism reveal differences as well as similarities. Such a state of affairs should not be at all surprising, given both the common grounding of the models in a diasporic phenomenon and the different character of the diasporas in question. Interestingly enough, the religious dimension is not one that I would foreground in this regard: despite our very different traditions and preoccupations, I find myself, on the whole, in agreement with Boyarin's interpretation of the Pauline agenda as universalist and coercive. Indeed, it is an agenda that I find quite harmful to the 'Greek' as well: I am a Christian, baptized into Christ, but I am also—at one and the same time and among other things—a Cuban, a Latin American and a non-Westerner as well as a Cuban–American, a US North American and a Westerner. Such a sense of 'disaggregated' identity is not one that I would care to dispense with, in any particular direction. In what follows I limit myself to those differences and similarities I consider most salient.

Certain differences come readily to mind. To begin with, Boyarin is specifically concerned with the Pauline literature, which he identifies as central to the Western tradition; I would argue for the need to look at the whole of the early Christian tradition, with a view of each and every text as a different, and perhaps even conflicted, ideological construction. In addition, Boyarin identifies within the Pauline literature a driving and interpretive hermeneutical center—the baptismal formula of Gal. 3.26-29 with its essentialist agenda of identity; I would argue for the need to look at the whole of the Pauline tradition, with a view of each and every letter as a different, and perhaps conflicted, ideological construction. Finally, Boyarin adopts a grand vision, along Hegelian lines, of the politics of identity from the first century onward—Christianity and Judaism as binomial opposites, with idealized diaspora as synthesis; I would argue for all sorts of representations of identity in the light of different texts, interpretations and interpreters.

Certain similarities come readily to mind as well. First, both Boyarin and I emphasize the need for critical dialogue with the texts of antiquity, their interpretations and interpreters: just as he sees such texts addressing him as a 'Jew', to borrow his own terms, so do I see them addressing me as a 'Greek' (and as a 'man' and as a 'freeman'). Similarly, both of us also emphasize the ideological dimension of such dialogue; moreover, despite his focus on identity and mine on geopolitics, I believe that we would both accept such angles of vision as not only central but also interrelated. Finally, both of us further regard the practice of criticism as an activity for liberation: against exclusivism and coercion, for justice and wellbeing.

It is against the background of these models that the essays in this volume stand and have their say. They too seek—sometimes favoring one task over the other, as signified by the Table of Contents—to reach a critical understanding of their own underlying diasporic realities and experiences and to advance a reading program in the light of such diasporic phenomena. These essays also constitute a harbinger of things to come: in the years ahead diasporic criticism will become increasingly popular and increasingly sophisticated. Indeed, it is safe to say that the phenomenon of self-conscious 'interpreting beyond borders' has only just begun.

## BIBLIOGRAPHY

Ashcroft, Bill, Gareth Griffiths and Helen Tiffin
1998        *Key Concepts in Post-Colonial Studies* (London: Routledge).
Barrett, David B. (ed.)
1982        *World Christian Encyclopedia: A Comparative Study of Churches and Religions in the Modern World, AD 1900–2000* (New York: Oxford University Press).
Boyarin, Daniel
1994        *A Radical Jew: Paul and the Politics of Identity* (Berkeley: University of California Press).
Boyarin, Daniel and Jonathan Boyarin
1993        'Diaspora: Generation and the Ground of Jewish Identity', *Critical Inquiry* 19: 693-725.
Connor, Walker
1986        'The Impact of Homelands upon Diasporas', in Gabriel Sheffer (ed.), *Modern Diasporas in International Politics* (New York: St Martin's Press): 16-46.

Crosby, Alfred W.
1986            *Ecological Imperialism: The Biological Expansion of Europe, 900–1900*
                (Cambridge: Cambridge University Press).
Safran, William
1991            'Diasporas in Modern Societies: Myths of Homeland and Return',
                *Diaspora: A Journal of Transnational Studies* 1: 83-99.
Segovia, Fernando F.
1995a           ' "And They Began to Speak in Other Tongues": Competing Modes
                of Discourse in Contemporary Biblical Criticism', in F.F. Segovia
                and M.A. Tolbert (eds.), *Reading from This Place*. I. *Social Location and
                Biblical Interpretation in the United States* (Minneapolis: Fortress Press):
                1-32.
1995b           'Toward a Hermeneutics of the Diaspora: A Hermeneutics of Other-
                ness and Engagement', in F.F. Segovia and M.A. Tolbert (eds.),
                *Reading from This Place*. I. *Social Location and Biblical Interpretation in
                the United States* (Minneapolis: Fortress Press): 57-73.
1995c           'Cultural Studies and Contemporary Biblical Criticism: Ideological
                Criticism as Mode of Discourse', in F.F. Segovia and M.A. Tolbert
                (eds.), *Reading from This Place*. II. *Social Location and Biblical Interp-
                retation in the United States* (Minneapolis: Fortress Press): 1-17.
1995d           'Toward Intercultural Criticism: A Reading Strategy from the Dias-
                pora', in F.F. Segovia and M.A. Tolbert (eds.), *Reading from This Place*.
                II. *Social Location and Biblical Interpretation in the United States* (Min-
                neapolis: Fortress Press): 303-30.
1998            'Biblical Criticism and Postcolonial Studies: Toward a Postcolonial
                Optic', in R.S. Sugirtharajah (ed.), *The Postcolonial Bible* (The Bible
                and Postcolonialism, 1; Sheffield: Sheffield Academic Press): 49-65.
1999            'Notes toward Refining the Postcolonial Optic', *Journal for the Study
                of the New Testament* 75: 103-14.
Subramaniam, Radhika
1996            'Diaspora', in Michael Payne (ed.), *A Dictionary of Cultural and Criti-
                cal Theory* (Oxford: Basil Blackwell): 144.
US Census Bureau
1995            'Population Projections of the United States by Age, Sex, Race and
                Hispanic Origin: 1995 to 2050'.
Walls, Andrew
1995            'Christianity in the Non-Western World: A Study in the Serial Nature
                of Christian Expansion', *Studies in World Christianity* 1: 1-25.

Part I

READING DIASPORA

# Gustavo Gutiérrez Goes to Disneyland: *Theme Park Theologies* and the Diaspora of the Discourse of the Popular Theologian in Liberation Theology

## Marcella María Althaus-Reid

In (Latin) America, the theologian is defined by her/his knowledge of the processes of liberation… It is very difficult in Latin America to conceive of a theologian reflecting at the margin of some engagement in the struggle for liberation, as has happened in Europe (Martínez Diez and García F. 1989: 56).

Six men play the leads in the grand opening of Haiti's incinerator. The six are burning as a punishment and as a lesson. They have buried the images of Christ and the Virgin that Fray Ramón Pane left them for protection and consolation. Fray Ramón taught them to pray…and to invoke the name of Jesus…[but] the [natives] buried the images because they were hoping that the gods would fertilise their fields of corn, cassava, boniato and beans (Galeano 1995: 69).

So where have all the 'natives' gone? They have gone between the defiled image and the indifferent gaze (Chow 1993: 54).

## Transversal Definitions

By 'Liberation Theology' I refer in this essay to the classical Latin American theology of liberation, with its universalist tendencies, as developed from the 1970s. Such theology is defined as a theological orthopraxis of economic and political liberation, contextualized in the experience of Latin American political and economic oppression and the struggle for social transformation and liberation. Traditionally, Liberation Theology had a limited hermeneutics of suspicion, although more recently cultural, sexual and racial elements have been incorporated. However, such incorporation seems to follow the conception of a linear theological journey, without the disruptions and fluctuations that a postcolonial hermeneutics would entail.

By 'Postcolonial Theology' I refer to the criticisms of that way of theologizing imposed by the Western world as theology. The postcolonial theological project shares elements of the liberationist one but problematizes such categories as 'the poor' and 'indigenous theology' because it is distrustful of the continuation of the Western ontology as the theoretical subject of theology.

By 'Diasporic Theology' I mean the postcolonial discourse that emphasizes the displacement or the erring in Liberation Theology as a sort of meta-postcolonial discourse characterized by identity in instability and geographical conflict. This is the place where we can discuss the conceptual joint construction of Liberation Theology from Latin America and the North Atlantic as a metadiscourse on the politics of deviancy in postcolonial Liberation Theology. Latin America is not the destiny (by geographical determination) of Liberation Theology but one of the many sites where the promiscuity of a disseminated theological discourse travels.

In this essay my aim is to engage in these three standpoints transversally, that is, opening up borderline points of agreement and departure and seeing how conceptualizations sometimes coexist even if in opposition. My objective is to reflect on the 'popular theologian' as the interpreter of the Bible in Latin America from a diasporic perspective, questioning the construction of his or her identity outside the colonial North Atlantic discourse of theological expectations. The popular theologian is not a person in diaspora but rather the conceptual product of Liberation Theology in the diaspora of the theological markets of Europe and the United States. Therefore, it is of utmost importance to clarify and reflect on the hybridity of the popular theologian trajectory in order to untangle the postcolonial project of interpretation 'of the word and the World'.

On Differences and *Différance*:
From Liberating Theology to Postcolonial Suspicion

The new gods of Fray Ramón Pane's story in the sixteenth century did not fertilize the soil of Abya-Yala.[1] No matter how many statues of Jesus and Mary the natives buried, no prosperity came for the children of the Sun God and the Mother Earth. Unfortunately, it was only their own native blood, poured out during the genocide of the Conquista that fertilized the land, bringing prosperity and untold riches to the Western Christian invaders. This was the sixteenth-century Gospel of European Prosperity, a gospel that the Roman Catholic Church in the renamed Latin American continent kept faithfully through centuries of alliances between church and state powers.

However, religious structures are symbolic figurations that change meaning according to the prevalent forces in the field of economic production. The crisis of the 1950s in Latin America, including the triumph of the Cuban Revolution in 1959, produced a change of consciousness in the continent's perception of both the ethos of theology and the role of the church in the continent. This was the beginning of the liberationist movement, which became prosperous in legends, because legend-making is part of the traditional way of cultural appropriation of the West. Legend-making was part of the process of understanding of the new theological thought coming from the South. Legends are made up of several stories unified by a male or female central character. The legend of the popular theologian as community theologian was drawn within a picturesque contrast involving, on the one hand, the community-committed, barefoot academic from the South reading the Bible with the poor and, on the other hand, the proper North Atlantic theologian made of books and university research. Unfortunately, the legend, wrapped with quasi-ontological

---

1.   Abya-Yala was the original name given by the Kuna of Panama to the continent called Latin America by the Conquista. Americus Vespucius was the conquistador who used his own name to name the continent. The emphasis in 'Latin' America obliterates the presence of African cultures, apart from the native cultures of the continent.

myths about Latin Americans and poverty, was set in a dynamic relation with liberationist discourse and ended up hybridizing it.[2]

The tension that arises in theology from knowledge and a some-times unrelated practical experience found a path of resolution in a new understanding of the theological role in Liberation Theol-ogy, but, once it received the acceptance of the Western theologi-cal market, the figure of the popular theologian permutated its own boundaries for the diasporic needs of Western academics in search of new identities. Although there is partial truth in saying that the popular theologians were opposed in their conceptualiza-tion and methodological frame to their North Atlantic counterp-arts, for the makers of easy discourses on liberation the reality has, unfortunately, been far more complex than this. The so-called split between Liberation theologians and North Atlantic theologians obeyed a dialectic not of *différance* but of differences in mutual dependency.

North Atlantic theology and Third World Liberation Theology may have a long history of differences, but not of *différances,* be-cause there is no deferral of meaning in theological praxis. *Différance* may have done theology with the buried statues of Christ and the Virgin Mary, while differences made an implicit theologi-cal contract based on agreements and compromises with the cen-tral (Western) discourse of faith. If it is right to say that there has been an epistemological difference in theology during the past 25 years, given the takeover of the traditional idealism of the West by a materialist methodology, it must also be acknowledged that the differences were not substantial but rather reconciliatory in nature. The popular theologian was the key figure in this process of adaptation whereby theology was not de-centred but relocated in the context of cultures of poverty. The narratives of the 'theolo-gian from the poor', the 'Christ of the poor', and 'theology from poverty' never de-centred Christian Western theology but rather adapted it more successfully. Indeed, the very possibility of divid-

2.    Here I use the concept of 'hybridity' following Mikhail Bakhtin's idea of the dialogic imagination constituted by the encounter of different linguis-tic consciousness. From the point of view of cultures, this thought is reflected in the idea that no theology is without transmutations, borrowings and appro-priations. Depending on the context, results may be subversive or supportive of the status quo (1981: 358-60).

ing theologies into two groups, such as 'bad ones' (North Atlantic) and 'good ones' (Third World Liberation), or vice versa, shows the degree of dualism in the discourse of the divine and historical scene in which this discourse is still grounded. Such dualism, in the long term, does not help the cause of liberation, because the mechanisms of dependency are perpetuated in repetitive models, Pavlovian models—a sort of resurrection paradigm of the Western style of obsessive classification and moralization of ideas and behaviours.

## Context: 'Theme Parks' of Theology

> Theology is returning to the hands of its true makers (Fraser and Fraser 1986: 46).

> Here youth may savour the challenge and promise of the future (Disneyland, Dedication Plaque, July 1995).

The discourses about the poor, with their constitutive dualism, have been contested in recent years, even within the inner circles of Liberation Theology. 'The poor' as the subject of Latin American theology functioned as a Metaphysics of Presence or abstract authority obliterating the contradictions that gender, sexuality and race introduce in the analysis of the poor masses. A metatheological discourse is now limiting universals while opening the liberationist understanding of reality. This metadiscourse is a form of postcolonial theology with elements of a diasporic theological critique which acknowledges that the conceptualization processes of Latin American Liberation Theology have never been as stable as the constructions done from Western academic circles wanted the public to believe.[3]

---

3.    The issue of Latin American theological identity in North Atlantic discourse follows the same rules of any process of essentializing colonial identities. The main characteristic is bodily (or geographical) fixation, which deauthorizes any contradictory sign of the fixed identity or mutations produced. The 'Otherness' of Liberation Theology is therefore an object of codification, seldom of disruption. An example of this is the discourse of 'the poor' and the photographs and artistic perceptions of 'the poor'. One may think that the poor in Latin America use uniforms, speak the same language, have the same beliefs, and look the same.

Postcolonial theologies go further than liberationist ones because their quest is to dehegemonize multiple bodies, such as
human bodies in the discursive limits of sexuality, for instance,
but also bodies of knowledge, including cultural and economic
knowledge. Liberationists share partially in the dehegemonization
process of the postcolonial project. A theology done from our
own people's cultures is at the root of this process, but the split
comes when Liberation Theology considers Western Christian faith
and the systematization of theology as a natural or given in the
process of doing theology. Liberationists are happy to find in the
Bible Christ as the liberator of the poor but not to accept the deconstruction of Christ the subject, who, in some forms of popular
religiosity in Latin America, emerges as a woman, the child of a
dying mother, a corpse who walks, or even multitudes instead of
an individual.[4] Moreover, there is the fact that sometimes Christ *is
not*, because the constructed Christian Christ has not been able to
join people's symbolic processes, to the point that it can no longer
be claimed to be compatible with traditional methodological
frames of understanding God. Such is the case, for instance, in a
theology of the Dirty War in Argentina, as it reflects on torture
and the function of euchariststic rituals in concentration camps
and detention centres (Graziano 1992). The Basic Ecclesial
Communities (BECs) show that liberationists can improve the
structures of the church but not replace them with traditional
indigenous forms of community religious organization or new al-
ternatives coming from the experience of workers, guerrilla movements or popular women's organizations.

Perhaps the most important thing to understand is that postcolonial theologies have unmasked the fact that Western theological discourse works by simulation. For instance, to simulate spiritual and structural Western reality among Latin Americans is a task
that accentuates hegemonic divine productions, such as theological discourses. However, Liberation Theologies have been forced
to participate in the simulation process in a subtle way, because
their ultimate authority still lies in the central church structures of
the West and in the academic centres of Europe and the United
States. From that perspective, Liberation Theology becomes a sort
of 'theme park' of theology, variously characterized as 'Latin

4.    For instance, in Argentina, *Santa Librada* is a female crucified Christ.

American' theology, 'Indigenous' Theology, or 'Latin American Women's' Theology. These are interesting theological subthemes worthy of being visited, and people in the West are encouraged to visit them as if going to a botanical garden. Such a theme park conception thwarts pluralism. It may be the theology of the poor, but it still obeys the tradition of the thinking and logic of the centre, and, although in opposition, it perpetuates the centre's discourse by default. It is the visitor to the theme park who carries meaning to the product. Moreover, the fact of being presented as a theme park accentuates the imaginary aspect of the construction of regional theologies. They highlight by their mere native presence the fact that real theologies are elsewhere, and, as such, may be called 'theologies at the margins' in more than one sense.

Liberation Theologies as theme parks function at the level of popular attractions and have done a lot for the book market of the Western world, as an extension of the capitalist market of theological production of goods. Crafts, fashion, books, food, posters and a collection of popular travel anecdotes have been marketed in Europe and the States as products of the 'theology of liberation'. All these productions work at the level of expressive symbols organized in the following way: The centrepiece of theological thinking is constituted by systematic Western theology, and it is done even if in opposition. The theme parks, in the case of Liberation Theology, are divided into subthemes, such as 'Marxist Theology', 'Evangelical Theology', 'Indigenous Theology', 'Feminist Theology'—all of them with a central unifying theme ending with 'and the poor'. The true makers of the future of Disneyland ideology and the true makers of theology as seen by the Frasers share a common illusion of being equals in a dream of being different.

## Capitalist Codes: A Key for a Further Analysis of Theological Theme Parks

Liberation Theology as a theme park theology is the natural context of the popular theologian. The Western understanding of productivity homologizes at a certain level the work of the popular theologian as the one who produces things with theological ideas. 'To produce things' means to continue with an understanding and approval of a system of theological production, but, since the concept of poverty used by Liberation Theology came from dependency theory, the popular theologian was defined as independent of church and state structures of control. This is the meaning of the concept of the theologian living among the poor.

The focus of this construction of the theologian's identity in Liberation Theology was political and cultural decentralization, with certain limits applied to the understanding of faith according to orthodoxy, classical church organization, and so forth. From there the image of the Roman Catholic priest or Protestant minister who lives with the poor and reads the Bible with them while engaged politically emerged powerfully not only in Latin America but also in Europe and in the United States. Stress was put on the simplicity of people's faith and community sharing of the Gospel and on how the popular theologian simply reflected that. At this point, the popular theologian's reflection was never his or her own but the people's reflection. The popular theologian was a mirror who reflected images from the poor, a mirror that 'gives a visible image to the invisible people' who were outside the theological market at the time. The relation of production was thus a peculiar one.

The popular theologian became the intermediary of the free market society, the parasite who gave 'a voice to the voiceless' as if without his or her presence the poor could not speak. That has never been the case in Latin America, but the fear of theological misconstructions lay behind the role of the popular theologians. Clodovis Boff wrote extensively about the risk of *bricolage*[5] or producing 'a carnival of meaning' by allowing poor people in the BECs to read the scriptures without the guidance of Christian (Roman Catholic) traditions and proper methodology (Boff and Boff 1987: 139). Such is Boff's terror of the voice of the voiceless that he demands that such popular readings of the Bible be done with a method he devised ('correspondence of relationship') and the continuous use of Church traditional teaching and herme-

5.    I have argued elsewhere that Boff misunderstood Claude Lévi-Strauss's concept of *bricolage*. For Lévi-Strauss it is a positive concept that expresses the multiplicity of materials to be used for a symbolic construction, but Boff interprets it negatively as a *vale todo* ('everything is valid'). This shows Boff's fear of multivocal theological dialogue and the failure of his liberation theological assumptions.

neutic tradition. Therefore, the popular theologian becomes the 'punk' whose father sells the safety pins punks use in their ears.

This is not to say that popular theologians did not have any genuine commitment to and engagement with social changes. Obviously, they did and still do, but these end with reformism or, to put it in another way, with the way we do the marketing of theology to include a vast public that was outside our reach. I have said elsewhere that no guerrilla group in Latin America has ever been called 'The Prophet Isaiah' or 'The Gospel of the Alternative Kingdom Movement', but rather *Tupac-Amaru, Tupamaros* or *Montoneros*—names associated with indigenous rebellious movements of no religious origin. However, this does not diminish the religious role of resistance and its importance for revolutionary movements, as far as its preoccupation is related not only to the self-perpetuation of a Western-based definition of what theology is and the role of the theologian but also to the underlying methodological and logical assumptions, which in reality are productive assumptions.

Unfortunately, a touristic theological industry existed and created much confusion, in the sense that this industry became part of an academic imaginary. However, my claim is that the popular theologian has been and still is real, but under permanent construction with regard to his or her role, and that it is important to analyse the mythological shift in that construction. The popular theologian has been and still is a priest or minister, living in poverty, doing community work in a slum while teaching in a seminary or working in a parish, and reflecting and acting with the people. Eventually, they might produce a book or not. I had lecturers in my own seminary in Buenos Aires during the early 1980s who performed all these roles at the same time, for little or no pay at all. They went to jail; they confronted the military state; they disappeared and suffered torture and death.

However, at the margins of life, there is a non-coincidental discourse, such as the academic one, that builds narratives like that of the popular theologian and not always in concordance with reality. The popular theologian, as a key classical performer of Liberation Theologian, is in reality a hybrid construction between native and European discourse, concerning not only the task of theology but the shifts of definitions from the modern to the postmodern paradigm. To call it 'hybrid' does not connote a pejorative meaning but indicates tensions in the construction of identity and fidelities. What we define today as a popular theologian has changed and has been transformed during the past ten years. More importantly still, this has been done mostly independently of the historical experience of popular theologians, such as Gustavo Gutiérrez. To observe and analyse such conceptual changes provides us with interpretive clues with which to understand elements in Liberation Theology that became more postcolonial than liberationist and, in the end, to identify how diasporic thought, as part of a metatheology of liberation, has challenged the scene even further.

However, we are not fully in the presence of a postcolonial or diasporic systematic theology. Postcolonial and diasporic theologies are of a dispersed nature, because, in essence, they are contrary to the more Western notion of systematizing theology. The point is precisely one of opening borders and tunnels under the theoretical constructions of the West, not only in the content of theology but also in challenging the order of submission that lies behind systematic theologies. In systematic theology we find the quasi-anthropological compulsion of the West for classifying a theory of understanding of God as theology into neat, closed compartments or systems. Is this administrative, taxonomic and colonial order in which historical experiences of some discourse about God and humanity are comprised challenged in postcolonialism and diasporic thought? If so, a reflection on the genesis of theological theme parks should provide us with important clues to consider.

Indeed, such genesis should be seen as a hybrid process. The discourse of the church is a process of production obeying the logic of the formation of capital. Theological categories like 'salvation' or 'revelation' are not disembodied universal truths, captured by some oracular or mediumistic communication with the Sacred but rather the fruit of labour. Moreover, such categories participate in a process of appropriation of labour and exploitation. In classical North Atlantic theology reflections have followed and have been followed by early assumptions from the industrial model.

Classical liberalism was rooted in a particular anthropology modelled after an atomistic nature. People's object in life, according to Jeremy Bentham, was a negation, the absence of labour and the following of pleasure, with pain and sacrifice to be avoided (1955: 341). The moving force for change was to be found only among the higher ranks in a classed society, with the individualistic rather than communitarian aspects of life to be stressed. Theology mirrored that, for I believe that political forces are stronger in modelling society than sacred ones. Thus, theological production stressed sacrifice, pain, individual virtues and, in economic terms, competition and not solidarity with the Other.

Processes of colonization, for instance, are about spiritual competence but also competition. Western Christianity was able to prove that the white race was superior in spiritual terms to other races. Western theology affirmed its identity in a discourse of 'we are the best', which also justified the pillage of the colonies and the fables concocted to explain economic dependency in our present century. Economic and spiritual competition are related discourses of identity, based on perceptions of human relations as competitive. Another element to highlight is Thomas Malthus's population theory in relation with what he thought was the danger of an excessive birth rate on the planet (1981: 179-81). This produced a theology of restriction of sexuality, particularly valid when used with the indigenous people. To be more specific, theology became an industrial enterprise for the production of goods of ideological sustenance as well as of financial sustenance. After all, churches are vast enterprises where capital is accumulated and invested for profit. The churches were the first place where the capital was given a sacred status.

## The Logic of Selling More (Theology) and Producing Less

From a Marxist analysis we can consider that capital accumulation equals the profit of production. In the unjust, exploitative market in which capital acquires a life of its own, the being of capital, as lucidly pointed out by Enrique Dussel in his essay about Marx as a theologian, is at a deeper level the being of a non-being (1993: 270). That non-being is that of the exploited person who produced it but became alienated from it and negated, because their working contribution to the making of the capital does not even give its value to the product. The value of a good lies in its utility and not in labour, that is, the work of the producers.

To which capital are we referring here? Systematic theology is the capital of the church: it contains the doctrine of God and an understanding of religious consciousness. It is the place of Orthodoxy. However, dogmatics is based on the historical experience of a community's exploitation and restriction of life under dualistic patriarchal assumptions. The implicit anthropology in Western theology comes from an interpretive methodology that excludes the roots of human pain and suffering. Any ontology or projected theo-logy (discourse about God) that has not confronted human alienation as a result of a patriarchal capitalist system has a systematic theology made of exploitation. As soon as the church's capital—that now defined as the experience of and quest for God of the exploited masses in the midst of class, racial and sexual struggles—discards its producers, it becomes an abstraction. The capital of the church's dogma is sacralized. For its preservation, multitudes have been sacrificed. Economic interests are tied to ideological ones. Theology becomes a product to sell, but not allowing new producers to come on the scene. No new creative process can occur, except those that somehow come from the original dogmatics and perpetuate its preservation. To sell more and to allow less production means to invest more directly in the capital and not in the people as producers. Thus, dogmatics becomes more ahistorical than transcendent, while method in theology follows a similar pattern.

Liberation Theology wanted to break this economic pattern of making theology as an ideological capital to serve the interest of the elite in power. This was also reflected in the structure of the churches and in their accumulation of material wealth in terms of lands, buildings and investments amid the poverty and destitution of the original producers of theology. Their product, that is, their experiences of God in the midst of a life of exploitation and degradation, was not only denied but turned against them by a theological exchange mechanism. For instance, hard work badly paid was exchanged for the promise of eternal life by the currency of humility and submission. The controllers of theological capital and the system of exchange needed to be challenged. At this point,

Liberation Theology started to develop the concept of the popular theologian.

*The Popular Theologian*

This was defined as someone who could reflect theologically with and from the experience of the exploited masses in Latin America. In reality, this had started before the Second Vatican Council in a movement called ISAL (Church and Society in Latin America), which had a Marxist political background and was supported by such important theologians as Rubem Alves and José Míguez Bonino. The point was that the theologian should never expropriate the theological praxis of the poor or encourage the alienation of their experiences into a reflection based on an exchange system of immaterial goods for the currency of exploitation, as in the oppressive forms of current theologies. The popular theologian was a Marxist revolutionary, with a praxis oriented toward social change and the compassion and empathy with the poor of such revolutionaries as Ernesto 'Ché' Guevara or Fidel Castro, who did not compromise for the liberation of the people. The theologian then was thought of as the person who worked with the people and reflected and acted with them for the transformation of society. During the late 1960s and early 1970s, that revolutionary figure was based on a Freirean model: the popular theologian as a 'conscientizer'.

It is not coincidental, then, that Liberation Theology, following the Freirean conscientization methodology based on the experience of work in rural areas, started to use a topographic vocabulary. The terms used were 'grass roots'; 'doing theology from below'; 'from the base'; 'with feet on the ground'; 'down to earth'; 'underdogs of history'; 'underground theology'; 'indigenous theologies' (referring to the so-called 'Indian' population of Latin American natives). This was due to the fact that liberationists started to define their work mostly in relation with the Latin American peasant population. This happened at a time when agrarian reform was high on the agenda of the programme for independence. However, if the popular theologian had been defined from the reality of the urban poor, then it would have used border vocabulary: 'margins'; 'slums' (*barriadas marginales*); 'street level'; and terms associated, for instance, with factories and industrial life. This may be one of the reasons why the popular theologian could not survive ideologically or physically in the cities, and, as in the case of guerrilla movements, was only successful in rural areas. The early Movement of Third World Priests working in cities was persecuted and exterminated, leaving little scope for the continuation of the *guerrillero-priest* role, except in the mountains, as in the case of Camilo Torres. Nevertheless, the priest in the mountains adopted more the role of a guerrilla fighter than a spiritual leader, which was not a popular model to follow, especially among Protestants, who had families dependent on their work.

The popular theologian was a man—for women theology was a forbidden area in Liberation Theology during the 1970s—working in a rural area in some form of conscientization process. However, the concept did not evolve on its own for long, since it became dependent on European theology. In Europe, as in the United States, Latin America has always been seen through the eyes of those who only see *pampas*, horses, *gauchos*, natives and jungles. The image of picturesque faithful Christian natives dressed in colourful attire and cultivating the soil while suffering much exploitation was attractive for European discourse. The faith of the simple people amid their suffering, their interest in the gospel, and the childlike qualities of the native Christian started to be exalted. This image Europe reproduced, especially through books and articles, but also crosses, posters and Christian memorabilia.

*Reading the Bible*
In academic circles the re-reading of the Bible done in the BECs was the key element to publicize. The popular theologian had acquired by now the role of the interpreter of the poor. However, contrary to this belief, the Roman Catholic Church did not encourage the reading of the Bible in the BECs; the Bible was used sparsely, because the BECs were constituted almost completely by illiterate people and the church had not promoted the Bible during its five hundred years of existence in Latin America. Carlos Mesters, one of the most honest voices regarding the truth of popular biblical readings, presents us with a picture of readings that were done sporadically and without a particular methodological option (1993: 15-16). This meant that the Bible was, at times, read as an oracle to divine the future, a talisman for good luck, an

allegory or literal truth. The allegorical form was approved by European academia, while the literalist forms were ignored.

In Latin America, popular theologians were conscious, as Mesters himself admits, of the risks of biblical interpretations done in a totally spontaneous way. Such spontaneity was mediated by messages received, for example, from the media, with unpredictable results. For instance, during the late 1970s, I participated in a popular Bible Study in Argentina, where a man claimed that Mary Magdalen, announcing the resurrection of Christ, was not only disbelieved by the apostles but also beaten by them. The minister intervened to read the Scripture again and to prove that this was not the case: Mary Magdalen had not been beaten. However, it transpired that a television drama based on the gospel had presented a scene where Mary Magdalen was slapped in the face by disbelieving apostles. Even if the Bible did not say so, people were adamant that 'they saw it happening'. When the minister intervened to say that God did not approve of men beating women, people counter-argued that perhaps the Bible was saying that it was fine to beat a woman only if she was considered to be a liar. Just as these interpretations were common, so there were also other forms of reading the Bible among the poor that were more of a dialogue regarding issues of daily life, with an occasional quotation from the Bible by the leader to illustrate the point.

There was little analysis of the role of the media among the poor and marginalized. The problem was that these Bible Studies were 'too loose' to be shown as examples of popular interpretation. Liberationists wanted popular readings that could be displayed as examples of the exegesis people could produce. Exegesis obviously depended on many factors, including the literacy level of a group, but the best examples, those that resulted in actions of liberation in the community, were, in general, not worth publishing. In other words, they could not pass the test of Western academia. Therefore, in academic circles, the popular theologian needed to be refashioned again as a leader, a guide in the process of people re-reading the Scriptures, although books and articles written at the time as 'authentic exegesis from the people' tended to obscure the intervention of the leader and stress spontaneity.

In Europe, that spontaneity was admired. Western academia saw the popular theologian as a benevolent father dealing with ignorant, although sweet and well-disposed, native children. Two discourses, one Latin American and the other European, started to produce the imaginary of the Latin American popular theologian, but in Europe that image was naive and simplistic. No wonder many Europeans tried to use this image to work in their own communities without result. However, it was stressed that the Latin American context was different because Latin American people were different. In popular biblical studies done in Europe, the Latin American native was, then, sadly missed. The European poor were not as simple and as grateful faithful Christians and did not produce the original exegesis of their Latin American counterparts. Many Europeans would have liked to have submissive, faithful Christian natives in their parishes, instead of real people. In Latin America, however, the discourse was more prudent. Excesses were only the product of confrontation with Europe and the necessity of self-affirmation. In Europe it was thought that there were thousands of popular theologians working with the poor—statistics that were obviously exaggerated, as Gustavo Gutiérrez has pointed out (Gibbs 1996: 369). The BECs did not have the elements to make a Disneyland film of them.

*The Popular Theologian: A New Definition*
Clodovis and Leonardo Boff produced a book in the late 1980s to help clarify this point. The popular theologian was not to be considered anymore the guerrilla priest. At the time, the guerrilla movement had been defeated and dictatorships in Latin America were giving way to a democratic transition. In their book *Introducing Liberation Theology* (1987), obviously aimed at Western students, popular theology is defined as a tree with three main branches: while the roots of the tree consist of the communities of the poor, theological reflection is carried on at three levels—the professional, the pastoral and the popular. It is interesting to notice that at the professional level theological discourse was defined as 'detailed and rigorous', while at the pastoral and popular levels it was considered to be 'organically related to practice...diffuse and capillary, almost spontaneous' (1987: 13).

Although the Boff brothers make the point that all three levels reflected on the same issues and that their work was interrelated, it becomes evident that the book was an effort to stress that the so-

called popular theologian should not be confused with the trained
academic, who used, according to the authors, 'the logic of eru-
dition', while the popular theologians used 'the logic of life'. Even
the location of the popular theologian needed to be specified.
During the 1970s, with the use of conscientization styles of work,
the locus of the popular theologian was the BECs; now, this
location was contrasted with the academic, as new theological
institutes based on Liberation Theology were opened in Latin
America. This shift in the conceptualization of the role of the liberation theologian came at the time of the critique of dependency
theory. Gutiérrez, in his revised edition of *A Theology of Liberation*
(Maryknoll, NY: Orbis Books, 1988), reflects on the impossibility
of keeping the categories centre and periphery, as they are too
simplistic and ignorant of the complexity of the struggle, but in
practice the shift was being produced in order to incorporate the
liberationist discourse into the proper realm of Western discourse.

Meanwhile, in Europe a number of books written by European
theologians doing their required tour of Latin American BECs
illustrate this incorporation while trying to keep the image of the
popular theologian as the prophet of the natives. For instance,
Christopher Rowland and Mark Corner, in their book *Liberating
Exegesis* (1990), present images from slides produced in Brazil
under the title of 'Parables of Today'. The popular theologian
emerges as the link between the sufferings of the community and
the world of politicians and paramilitary forces. The context is the
state terrorism of Latin America during the 1970s.

In the slides the popular theologian assumes different presentations: a young white man ('the parish priest') and an older, white,
European-looking man called 'the Bishop'. The bishop is responsible for ordaining a man from the community (who looks racially
ambiguous, but more on the side of a white Brazilian than a black
one). The bishop and the priest show how they are able to per-
form more roles than reading the Bible with the poor, such as
helping people out of jail, but they look very erudite, serious and
well educated (1990: 9). Both bishop and priest use glasses (probably to show that they know how to read) and are power figures.
There is almost a coolness in the image of the bishop, in contrast
to the community people portrayed. Bishop and priest show knowledge and political influence; they are almost Western academic

figures who command multitudes not by producing books but people—people whom they organize in popular demonstrations after they have taught them the meaning of the gospel. Even the political forces of the country bow to them and seem to release prisoners at their suggestion.

Rowland and Corner do not exercise any hermeneutics of suspicion in their reading of biblical interpretation in Latin America, especially from a postcolonial perspective. They do not step outside the theme park theology, perhaps because outside the land feels uncomfortable and contradictory. Basically, Liberation Theology in action has always been diasporic and unsettled, more in tune with Chaos Theory than with North Atlantic systematic theology.

*The Prophetic Model: Problematic*

All this reflects the 'prophetic model', which followed the hierarchical and authoritarian tradition of the church. This was not, of course, a new model for the church in Latin America, which is the church of the 'cross and sword' and the sustainer of political, cultural and religious Western imperialism. How can a theologian be popular in a church that was authoritarian even in its propheticness? During the 1970s, the continent was living under the harshest forms of dictatorial powers, whose authoritarian claims could not be challenged or discussed. Part of the Roman Catholic Church confronted human rights violations, but did so through another authoritarian discourse, the prophetic one.

Liberationist discourses acknowledged cultural, economic and political domination from the West, but ignored the way domination was structured theologically. That is the point of prophetic models: they do not challenge theological structures to their root. Liberationists analysed the forms of theological discourses of oppression but ignored the structure of Western theological thought. Thus, the popular theologian, for instance, reverted to a discourse of theological efficacy without analysing which theological givens, or epistemological assumptions, were obstacles to such efficacy. For the church, the Christians who died in the struggle became martyrs. Thinking in terms of martyrdom is another example of theological Western incorporation in Liberation Theology. The central model was still that of North Atlantic Theology. Martyrdom was testimony, but there is a conceptual difference between 'martyrs' and *guerrilleros heroicos* (heroic guerrillas). In popular Catholicism, martyrdom participates in the category of resignation and sacrificial needs; it is not as positive or mobilizing as heroism. The point is that, while political militants tried to find models in a Latin American culture based in role models from the Conquista, Liberation Theology was busy readapting the teaching from the centres of Western theology.

## The Systematic Discourse of Popular Theologians

The problem was that the aura of illegality surrounding the liberationist process, as it organized a hermeneutical theology around systematic theology and capital formation, fascinated North Atlantic academia. Both Europe and the United States became romantically involved with the forces of production of Liberation Theology, which can be defined as the BECs and the gatherings for the popular reading of the Bible. North Atlantic theology behaved as a paterfamilias, either disputing the insufficient knowledge of the natives or finding their childlike faith enchanting. In one way or the other, North Atlantic Theology did not let liberationists go their way freely.

Liberationists, meanwhile, wanted to be recognized as adults on an equal footing with their colleagues abroad. This was the moment of apologetics—a style very much overdeveloped by the Universidad de Centro América (UCA) in El Salvador, still in vogue today. Indeed, recent published work, such as the *Mysterium Liberationis* and the *Systematic Theology* of Jon Sobrino and Ignacio Ellacuría (1993, 1996), show the desire to be seen as equals and not different in the sense of *différance*. Both books claim that Liberation Theology is a proper systematic theology and, while different methodologically speaking, comparable in the end to North Atlantic Theology. And that is precisely the problem with a theology that was generated from a borderline, subversive edge, but was unable to transgress that border.

For the Western academic, this may be an example of Rey Chow's claim that desire is always located in the Other (1993: 32). The Western theologian projected a 'lack' in the making of the theme park of theology and the construction of the popular theologian. The hard movement of pushing frontiers in theology became an entertainment for an European public looking for novelty in the religious market but also for meaning. Theologians were looking for a meaningful framework of praxis for their lives, and through the alliance of a transverse conceptualization between Latin Americans and North Atlantic academics the theme park of liberation was produced.

Christianity is an utopia, and the actual process of utopia-making is basically diasporic, made of identity shifts at different levels but basically at the level of differentiating desires. The so-called decline of Liberation Theology at the moment, as assessed by European academics, may be no more than a decline in the market for the selling of books on Liberation Theology. But more than that it may be that the entertainment is over, because the constructed utopia of liberation is not, in the real world, the coherent narrative that theology wants. When Westerners sent Gutiérrez to Disneyland, they also became liberation theologians, traditionally dressed with their colonial vision of the poor in Latin America and the role of popular theologians.

Meanwhile, the real poor in Latin America have become totally excluded by the globalization processes and refuse to continue supporting BECs and popular Bible Studies. A tremendous diaspora of whole communities living in the streets, under bridges, desperately trying to cross frontiers looking for a job to give them food and shelter or to save their lives as people in Chiapas, cannot remain in any confined space of theology. This diaspora is not an exodus: the point is one of multiple trespasses, over borders of economic, philosophical and political systems to understandings of sexuality and genderization of power and authority. This is not Liberation Theology but Postcolonial Theology, with a clear vocation for diasporic instability and sympathy for subversion more than for God. However, the challenges of theological hybridity are devastating for church and theology. And that is the good thing, because a postcolonial theology is not one that asks for the right to give a voice to the voiceless but that challenges the 'small voice' of Western theology in Liberation Theology as structurally part of Western Christianity and a discourse of the centre.

The Theology of Liberation is a hermeneutical theology. The reading of the Bible from a materialist perspective has been dependent on an understanding of the role of the popular theologian as part of the communities of the poor. Diasporic studies are crucial here to help us to discern the colonial dynamics of our Third World theological reflection. For instance, such studies can help us to denaturalize the whole theological enterprise, allowing us to see Third World theologies in their ambivalence and reflective bifurcations, which come not only from people's diasporas but also conceptual diasporas. The diaspora of the popular theologian is both internal and external. It challenges us with issues of the representability of the culture of poverty in theology and the translation process that is at the core of liberationist thought, usually expressed with the phrase 'to give voice to the voiceless'. However, Gayatri Spivak has warned us against benign representations of the subaltern in colonial thought and the validity of representation once the subaltern has moved to the area of representation at the cost of their alienation (1993: 90). The popular theologian is the 'alienated intermediate' figure in the reading of the Bible, representing the interface between Occidental theologies (North Atlantic) and Oriental theologies (Third World).

However, the concept of the popular theologian shows fluctuations and degrees of incoherence during the course of its development that can be encouraging, if we consider that the subversive force present is the one resisting systematization. The subversive power is present by the mechanism of exaggeration and negation. The theme parks of theologies are a diasporic product based on this dialectic of 'negation/exaggeration'. What is exaggerated in the North Atlantic shows the degree of 'colonial enlargement' in the limitations or lack thereof regarding community life in Latin America. Typical of this discourse is the affirmation by negation present in such common phrases as: 'the Latin Americans are communitarian people, not individualists like us', 'they are faithful, not secular as we are', or 'these people are humble and not competitive as we are'. What is exaggerated in Latin America also shows exaggeration but based on a mimicry of European Theology. This mimicry constitutes our colonial souls, arising from a process of identity based on negation of the non-colonial. This is the discourse of the children of Wesley and Calvin, not of the indigenous Christianity of the continent. From the contradictions and fluctuations that a diasporic reflection throws into the construction of the popular theologian, we rescue its phantasmatic nature as a crucial site of subversion. The popular theologian had been made to mediate between negations and exaggerations, but it is not more than a phantasmatic figure. It is a spectre of the 'something else' needed in Western theology, but also a domesticator of our colonial souls and a new colonial border of theology. This is a point of resistance and delegitimization by the deconstruction of the negation/exaggeration paradigm.

Finally, to discern the genesis of the popular theologian and the spectre of her/his reality would always be a major contribution to popular biblical interpretation in Latin America and a key point of reflection on the colonial tensions of our more autochthonous theological discourses, even if it is no more than a place of resistance. Paraphrasing Régis Debray in his interview of Subcomandante Marcos in Chiapas, the end of utopias is not a surrendering, but resistance must not cease (Debray 1996: 137). Resistance in Latin America is always the privileged site of a return to the essential of our Latin American discourse on politics and biblical interpretation in the diaspora of a theological discourse that went to Europe and came back to us as a hybrid product of different dreams and struggles.

## BIBLIOGRAPHY

Bakhtin, Mikhail
    1981        *The Dialogic Imagination* (Austin: University of Texas Press).
Bentham, Jeremy
    1955        'An Introduction to the Principles of Morals and Legislation', in
                A. Melden (ed.), *Ethical Theories* (Englewood Cliffs, NJ: Prentice–
                Hall [1789]).
Boff, Leonardo, and Clodovis Boff
    1987        *Introduction to Liberation Theology* (Maryknoll, NY: Orbis Books).
Chow, Rey
    1993        *Writing Diaspora* (Indianapolis: Indiana University Press).
Debray, Régis
    1996        'Talking to the Zapatistas', *New Left Review* 218: 128-37.
Dussel, Enrique
    1993        *Las metáforas teológicas de Marx* (Estella: Verbo Divino).
Fraser, Ian, and Margaret Fraser
    1986        *Wind and Fire: The Spirit Reshapes the Church and Basic Christian Com-
                munities* (Dunblane: Basic Communities Resource Centre).

Galeano, Eduardo
 1995        *Memory of Fire* (London: Quartet Books).
Gibbs, Philip
 1996        *The Word in the Third World: Divine Revelation in the Theology of Jean-
             Marc Éla, Aloysius Pieris and Gustavo Gutiérrez* (Roma: Pontificia Uni-
             versitá Gregoriana).
Graziano, Frank
 1992        *Divine Violence: Spectacle, Psychosexuality and Radical Christianity in the
             Argentine Dirty War* (San Francisco: Westview Press).
Gutiérrez, Gustavo
 1988        *A Theology of Liberation: History, Politics and Perspectives* (London: SCM
             Press).
Martínez Diez, Felicísimo, and Benjamín García F.
 1989        *La teología de la liberación es latinoamericana* (Caracas: Paulinas).
Malthus, Thomas
 1991        *Essays on the Principle of Population*, II, (New York: Dutton [1798]).
Mesters, Carlos
 1993        'The Use of the Bible in Christian Communities of the Common
             People', in N. Gottwald and R. Horsley (eds.), *The Bible and Libera-
             tion. Political and Social Hermeneutics* (Maryknoll, NY: Orbis Books).
Rowland, Christopher, and Mark Corner
 1990        *Liberating Exegesis. The Challenge of Liberation Theology to Biblical Studies*
             (London: SPCK).
Sobrino, Jon, and Ignacio Ellacuría (eds.)
 1993        *Mysterium Liberationis: Fundamental Concepts of Liberation Theology*
             (Maryknoll, NY: Orbis Books).
 1996        *Systematic Theology. Perspectives from Liberation Theology* (Maryknoll:
             Orbis Books).
Spivak, Gayatri
 1993        'Can the Subaltern Speak?', in P. Williams and L. Chrisman (eds.),
             *Colonial Discourse and Post-Colonial Theory: A Reader* (Hemel Hemp-
             stead: Harvester Wheatsheaf).

# Reading-Across: Intercultural Criticism and Textual Posture

## FERNANDO F. SEGOVIA

For the last few years I have been engaged in the conceptualization and articulation of a critical stance and program from the
diaspora, grounded in my own experience and reality of the diaspora and touching upon all of my various activities as a critic—literary, religious and cultural—within the context of the academy.
This task has led me in a variety of different though interrelated
directions: as literary critic, I have pursued the historical development and discursive configurations of Biblical Studies as a discipline; as religious critic, I have foregrounded the constructive
character of Religious Studies as a field, with a focus on Christian
Studies in general and on contemporary Theological Studies in
particular; as cultural critic, I have highlighted issues of construction, representation and power by turning to that contextual and
ideological analysis distinctive of the congeries of studies known as
Cultural Studies. The present essay represents a further step in my
elaboration of this diasporic project, with a focus on literary criticism.

In tracing the path and discourses of biblical criticism, I have
also advanced a theoretical model and reading strategy based on
my own diasporic experience and reality of exile. As point of
departure for this study, a brief summary of its central tenets thus
far is in order. In terms of model, I have argued for a hermeneutics of otherness and engagement: a view of texts, readings of texts
and readers of texts as others—not to be bypassed, overwhelmed
or manipulated but rather to be acknowledged, respected and engaged (Segovia 1995b). In terms of strategy, I have opted for intercultural criticism: an approach to texts, readings of texts and

readers of texts as literary or aesthetic, rhetorical or strategic and ideological or political products—not only to be analyzed as others but also to be critiqued in dialogue (Segovia 1995d). I have further linked both model and strategy to the geopolitical problematic of Postcolonial Studies: an approach to texts, readings of texts and readers of texts in terms of their respective imperial–colonial formations (Segovia 1998). In this present study, then, I should like to take a closer look at the strategy of intercultural criticism.

In effect, I should like to compare it with other reading strategies coming to the fore at this time and striving to take seriously into consideration the irruption of the real reader in interpretation. In so doing, I focus in particular on the attitude toward the text implicit in intercultural criticism—its posture of reading-across—in the light of the various postures offered, implicitly or explicitly, by such other strategies. That a variety of such strategies and attitudes should arise at this point should come as no surprise. Such proposals reflect, directly or indirectly, the impact of Cultural Studies on the discipline: on the one hand, the desire for new approaches to interpretation, given a profound and widespread dissatisfaction with regard to established methods and postures; on the other hand, the variety of such approaches, given the inevitable imprint of the ever more diversified world of criticism today.

My aim in this comparative study is twofold: to establish a sense of the overall spectrum regarding such strategies and attitudes and to situate intercultural criticism and reading-across within this spectrum. I shall proceed in three steps: I begin by examining that strategy and attitude that serve as point of departure for all such proposals and contrasting my own posture of reading-across within intercultural criticism; I then go on to examine a representative field of such proposals, differently grounded in modernism and postmodernism; finally, I proceed to locate my own proposal critically within such a spectrum.

## Reading-Of and Reading-Across: Scientific Criticismand Intercultural Criticism

All such proposals, including my own, stand against a common background: the reading strategy that has permeated not only traditional historical criticism but also literary as well as sociocultural criticism. A twofold word of clarification is in order, given my earlier comparison of the critical principles at work in these paradigms (Segovia: 1995a). First, I use the term 'reading strategy' here in a broad rather than narrow sense: the reference is not to matters of textual unity or rupture and their corresponding holistic or layered approaches to the text, as in that earlier comparison, but rather to an overall constellation and deployment of critical features. The result is 'reading strategy' writ large—what one might call a reading approach, a type of reading, a reading program or project. Second, while not ignoring similarities among the paradigms, it was the differences that I stressed in that earlier comparison. Here it is the similarities that I emphasize, in contradistinction to those critical features that underlie Cultural Studies.

*Reading-Of: Scientific Criticism*
The constellation and deployment of such similarities yield what I would call the 'scientific' type of reading, marked by the following fundamental characteristics:

a. An empiricist stance: texts were to be approached as realities 'out there' and thus as having preexisting, stable as well as determinate, and guiding or controling meaning—'original meaning' —which meaning may derive from the text itself, from the author(s) of the text, from the world of the text or any combination thereof.

b. An objectivist gaze: the texts 'out there' could only be deciphered 'from here' by a 'scientific' type of reading, whereby readers would put aside their 'prejudices' as human subjects (avoiding 'eisegesis') and thus uncover or recreate, in 'objective and disinterested' fashion, textual meaning (engaging in 'exegesis').

c. A hierarchical bias: 'scientific' reading demanded a highly informed and universal reader, ultimately grounded, if not actually situated, in the academy and trained according to well-established and rigorous principles of research and analysis.

d. A competitive strain: in their objective search for original meaning, highly informed and universal readers proved invariably at odds on any point of interpretation and accounted for such discrepancies and disagreements on the basis of incomplete or defective analysis, to be duly pointed out and corrected.

Only upon proper subscription to and exercise of such critical principles, therefore, could the meaning of the text be uncovered and recreated, to the extent allowed by the sources. Again, this type of reading applied whether the optic in question was of a historical (text as means), literary (text as medium), or sociocultural (text as means and medium) sort.[1]

In that earlier comparison of critical principles (Segovia 1995a), I dealt with six categories of analysis in all: location of meaning; reading strategy; theoretical foundations; the role of the reader; theological presuppositions; pedagogical implications. A further such principle can be readily added: attitude or posture toward the text.

In the case of scientific reading, silence before the text was imperative.[2] Scientific reading called upon its operative reader-construct, the informed and universal critic of the academy, to refrain from taking any type of stand with regard to the text under consideration. The task of the critic was to uncover or recreate the meaning of the text—whether posited in the text or in the author or the world behind the text—not to express any sort of reaction, cognitive or affective, or any sort of evaluation, positive or negative, regarding the text. For scientific reading, therefore, the aim of criticism lay solely in the recuperation and exhibition of data

1.   I have argued (Segovia 1995c) that certain developments within both literary and sociocultural criticism prepared the way for the interjection of the real reader in cultural studies, such as the concern with multiple interpretations and intratextual readers in literary criticism and the focus on socioeconomic and sociocultural identity of readers in sociocultural criticism. My point is that by and large it was scientific reading that predominated in these paradigms.

2.   This is true, though in different ways, of what could be characterized as two major strands in scientific criticism: a majority tendency toward a hermeneutics of trust—a view of the text as reliable; a minority tendency toward a hermeneutics of suspicion—a view of the text as biased. While in the former strand the text in question is that of the ancient narrative, in the latter it is that of the narrative of the 'text' posited behind the ancient text. The hermeneutics of suspicion is most evident in the historical criticism of the nineteenth century. See Barton (1998), who argues for a preponderance of trust based on underlying ecclesiastical concerns and commitments and calls for a vital renewal of suspicion-based criticism. My representation of scientific criticism in this section reflects the predominant strand of trust.

from antiquity, not in engagement and dialogue with such data—not in the public arena anyway.[3] That task would be left for others to pursue, 'theologians' of any stripe, who would nonetheless be expected to rely on the fruits of such detached scholarly research, if they were to be taken seriously. With regard to the text, therefore, scientific criticism was, at least in theory, far more descriptive than analytical—a posture that I would characterize as 'reading-of'.

This critical stricture of silence continued, to be sure, the traditional policy of keeping the real reader out of the interpretive process. Yet, such a stricture was not, in principle, sacrosanct. A violation of it would not necessarily have been seen as incurring 'eisegesis' but would have been certainly perceived as unseemly, precisely because it signifies the undesirable intromission of the flesh-and-blood reader into the critical discussion. Thus, even if such an insertion took place only after the process of exposition, of uncovering and recreating, had come to an end, it was to be avoided as lying beyond the proper purview of the 'exegete'. Even if technically correct, such a move would always represent a setting aside of the critical mask of objectivity and universality that grounded the whole critical experience.[4]

From the perspective of Cultural Studies, this attitude of silence can only be described as highly problematic. First, because such a posture allowed what were highly personal and social constructions, containing implicit reactions and evaluations of all sorts at every step of the way, to pass as solid and impartial 'scientific' findings. In other words, the meaning of the text thus re-'created' and the world of the text thus re-'constructed' failed to be seen and presented as constructions of antiquity on the part of positioned and interested readers. In the eyes of Cultural Studies, the result

3. In the suspicion-based strand, the search for 'truth' leads to the establishment of the 'facts' that lie behind the 'biased' texts. Such an approach certainly takes a stand regarding the text, indeed against the text, but only to establish a 'text' of its own—an underlying and true narrative. In so doing, it breaks the posture of silence vis-à-vis the text, but only to uncover and recreate historical 'truth' and thus engage in the further recuperation and exhibition of data from antiquity. In the end, silence vis-à-vis the newly established 'text' continues.

4. This would be true as well of suspicion-based criticism, since the reader-construct at work is not a real reader but an informed and universal critic.

was not a representation of antiquity but a re-*presentation*. Second, because such a posture let the rhetoric and ideology of the text, as constructed, stand untouched and hence secure. Since criticism did not involve critique, the text, as 'text' and 'history', remained impervious to any sort of critical commentary or judgment regarding its strategic concerns and aims as well as its ideological stance and consequences. Consequently, scientific reading, with its attitude of reading-of, could not but serve to reinforce the authority of the text as interpreted by its readers, and thus ultimately the authority of such readers and their readings as well.[5]

As such, it was a type of reading best described as apolitical on the surface. If the political entered at all into the discussion—subordinated as it always was to the theological—it was only at the level of the text or of the world behind the text and always by way of description, hardly at the level of interpretation and interpreters, of readers and readings, or by way of critique. From the perspective of Cultural Studies, with its foregrounding of context and ideology at every level, such a seemingly apolitical reading was not only highly illusory but also highly political. First, insofar as it kept its own location and agenda closely under guard; second, insofar as it let the force of the text, as uncovered and recreated, hold sway in the process. For scientific reading, therefore, the option for textual silence was never regarded, much less analyzed, as a critical and political move in its own right.

*Reading-Across: Diasporic Reading*
It is only with the advent of Cultural Studies, as the construct of the informed and universal reader yields to that of the real reader, that scientific reading and textual silence begin to be examined and evaluated as both strategy and attitude, as critical options rather than givens. Out of such revisioning, other types of reading and textual attitudes have begun to emerge, including my own

5.    Such critique would apply to suspicion-based criticism as well: not only would the underlying 'text' be offered as a solid and impartial 'scientific' finding rather than as a re-presentation of antiquity, but also the rhetoric and ideology of such a 'text' would stand untouched and secure rather than subject to critique. Here, insofar as the authority of the text yields to the authority of the underlying 'text' posited, the authority of readers and their readings is enormously reinforced.

program of intercultural criticism and posture of reading-across. In the past I have dealt with intercultural criticism at length but not so with reading-across. The two options, however, are highly interrelated and interdependent.

Situated within Cultural Studies, both stand on a very different set of critical principles than those of scientific reading and reading-of, insofar as they seek to move beyond empiricism, objectivism, hierarchism and competitiveness:

a. Against empiricism, texts are viewed as realities 'out there' (material and linguistic signifiers, by and large preceding and outlasting real readers) but as having no meaning (linguistic and discursive signified) without readers: meaning is neither fully preexisting nor stable and determinative nor guiding and controlling.

b. Against objectivism, meaning is regarded as the result of an encounter between positioned and interested texts and positioned and interested readers, with the latter as the inevitable filter of the former: there is no objective and disinterested process of recuperation and exhibition.

c. Against hierarchism, all such encounters—and types of encounters or traditions of reading—are considered worthy of analysis and critique in their own right: the reading of the informed and universal reader in the academy represents but one tradition of reading, as positioned and interested as any other, both individually or collectively.

d. Against competitiveness, a multiplicity of meaning is posited as not only inevitable but also foundational: the attempt to secure a final and definitive meaning in the face of incomplete or defective approximations emerges as pointless.

Given such principles, intercultural criticism calls for a view of and approach to texts, readings of texts and readers of texts as aesthetic, strategic and political constructs. This reading program in turn cannot but yield a very different attitude toward the text, and thus reading-across calls for engagement and dialogue in lieu of exhibition and silence.

As such, both options embody the élan of diaspora hermeneutics, with its combined search for the otherness of the text and engagement with such otherness. On the one hand, the search demands that such otherness be acknowledged and respected. Intercultural criticism complies by analyzing the text as a literary, rhetorical and ideological construct. On the other hand, the engagement calls for evaluation and critique of such a construct. Reading-across complies by passing judgment on the construct, a judgment that comprehends aesthetic layout, strategic aims and political agenda. Indeed, the very conception of the text as a construct—a product advancing, within a given context, a particular stance, with recourse to certain techniques of argumentation as well as certain features of representation—demands an active and sharp questioning of such a construct. While such questioning does encompass narrative as well as rhetorical features, its focus lies above all on the ideological features of location and agenda.

Both options further embody the élan of diaspora hermeneutics insofar as they extend the search for otherness and engagement not only to texts but also to readings and readers of texts, since a text is always a 'text' or interpreted text—a reading that is in itself a literary, rhetorical and ideological construct and that is produced, in turn, by a reader who is a literary, rhetorical and ideological construct as well. Such 'texts' or reading-constructs and their producers or reader-constructs must likewise be established and engaged as others. While intercultural criticism undertakes an analysis of both constructs, reading-across proceeds to a critique in terms of aesthetic layout, strategic aims and political agenda. In this view, therefore, readings and readers of texts also advance, within given contexts, particular stances, on the basis of certain techniques of argumentation and certain features of representation. Consequently, they too must be subject to active and sharp questioning, a questioning that encompasses literary and rhetorical features to be sure but that concerns itself first and foremost with the ideological features of location and agenda.

For reading-across, therefore, the process of questioning, of evaluation and critique, is central. The imperative attitude before texts, readings and readers is not critical silence but critical dialogue. The voice of the real reader is not to be muted but foregrounded. Such a posture immediately raises, of course, the question of criteria: on what basis will such a process of evaluation and critique be undertaken? Here the question of who stands to benefit and who stands to lose from any construction becomes fundamental. At the same time, reading-across acknowledges a multiplicity of stances from which to evaluate and critique, just as intercultural criticism presupposes a multiplicity of approaches, of methods and models. The criteria for evaluation and critique are construed, therefore, not as fixed and universal but as situated and interested. In other words, the fundamental question of who stands to benefit and who stands to lose can be postulated from a variety of different perspectives. My own proposal I have constructed with a vision of liberation in mind:

a. In general, such liberation is envisioned for marginalized and oppressed groups—it is a liberation grounded in the acknowledgment of and respect for the otherness of those whose very otherness is overwhelmed and manipulated. From this perspective, it becomes imperative to see what texts, readings of texts and readers of texts serve to enhance or impede the task of liberation within their own contexts. This is a vision based on my own experience of the denial of otherness in the diaspora.

b. More specifically, such liberation is postulated within the geopolitical world of imperialism and colonialism—it is a liberation grounded in acknowledgment of and respect for the otherness of those who are subjugated, exploited and denigrated as the 'other' of empire. From this perspective, it becomes imperative to see how texts, readings of texts and readers of text stand with regard to their own respective imperial formations. This is a vision based on my own experience of colonial and neocolonial otherness.

Reading-across cannot remain content, therefore, with analyzing how texts, readings, and readers stand with regard to life in the world in general and life in an imperial world in particular, but must go on to evaluate and critique such positions in the light of its own stance regarding life in the world and life in the geopolitical world. In so doing, it reads 'across' the texts, readings and readers it analyzes in 'inter'-cultural criticism, highlighting what it considers liberative and rejecting what it considers oppressive. In so doing, it inserts the voice of the real reader, as constructed, into the discussion fully and unapologetically so. Criticism ceases to be a matter of recuperation and exhibition and becomes a matter of ethics and politics.

## Spectrum of Strategies and Attitudes

For the comparative exercise I draw on three proposals recently advanced; in so doing, I proceed in chronological fashion, not in terms of publication but rather of critical formation. I begin with the 'reading-with' of Gerald West, a proposal grounded in liberation hermeneutics—a classic example of modernism by way of counterdiscourse. Subsequently, I turn to the androcritical reading of Daniel Patte, a proposal rooted in literary semiotics—a perfect example of postmodernism by way of its predominant Western mode, poststructuralism. I conclude with the dialogical imagination of Kwok Pui-lan, a proposal grounded in global hermeneutics—a sharp example of postmodernism by way of its predominant non-Western mode, postcolonialism.

*Reading-With: Gerald West*
The first proposal, from Gerald West of the University of Natal, belongs within the framework of traditional liberation hermeneutics—a socioeconomic hermeneutics with direct and explicit reference to the context of South Africa, both in general and in particular, given its specific reference to KwaZulu-Natal.[6] To understand its wherefore and élan, an understanding of its proposed context is in order, drawn in a combination of socioreligious and sociopolitical terms.

From a socioreligious perspective, the context is represented as follows: First, the Bible functions as a significant text in South Africa—a text that has shaped and continues to shape its history and thus a text that has played a central role in the lives of many. Second, the Bible also functions as an ambiguous text in South Africa—a text that has been used for both oppressive and liberating ends, that is, for and against apartheid. Third, among the poor and marginalized, the Bible has functioned and continues to function as a symbol of the presence of the God of Life in their midst.

From a sociopolitical perspective, the context is further constructed as follows: First, South Africa has experienced a prolonged and profound political and interpretive crisis. Second, at present the political crisis has been resolved in principle, but the interpretive crisis has deepened. While prior to the political settlement the church functioned as a site of struggle, giving rise in the process to new readings and theologies, since then the church has begun

---

6.    I am relying primarily on two featured presentations of speaking-with (1996, 1998). For broader background, see his two larger works (1995, 1999).

to confront calls to put aside this mode of struggle. Third, the struggle for full life is by no means over, especially for the poor and marginalized, and thus the church must continue to foster and develop such new readings and theologies, making possible thereby 'the recognition and articulation of the subjugated and incipient resources of our struggle' (West 1996: 23).

Consequently, in the light of a political struggle that remains very much unfinished and in process, West calls for a renewed and ongoing commitment to a hermeneutics of liberation—a hermeneutics that foregrounds those most in need of life, the poor and marginalized. Moreover, since the Bible is looked upon by the poor and marginalized as both a symbol of God's presence and life among them and as the basic source of theology—much more so than any other source—such communities must be not only foregrounded but also involved in the process of interpretation. What is needed, therefore, is neither a 'listening to' nor a 'speaking for' but rather a 'speaking with' the poor and the marginalized. Although deeply rooted in its South African context, this proposal also follows the basic pattern of liberation hermeneutics; indeed, as West himself acknowledges, the process envisioned could be carried on—and is being carried on—anywhere in the world. Thus, beyond its specificity in South Africa, the proposal admits of universal application, involving poor and marginalized communities anywhere.

The interpretive process envisioned encompasses a number of constitutive features: the attitude of the poor and the marginalized toward the Bible; the relationship between popular reading and critical reading; the demands and mechanics of speaking-with; and the intended results of speaking-with.

To begin with, the poor and the marginalized are described as in possession of a quintessentially positive attitude toward the Bible. Despite its use as an instrument of death, oppression and exploitation against them, they continue to hold on to it and to use it on their behalf: for them the Bible represents life in the midst of death, liberation in the midst of oppression, justice in the midst of exploitation. The Bible lends meaning and hope to their world. The corollary of this attitude, though it remains largely unstated here, is that in the Bible the poor and the marginalized encounter a God who identifies with them and who works on their behalf and hence a God with whom they can identify and whom they can follow in their struggle for life, liberation and justice.

Second, the relationship between common readers and academic readers is said to begin at the behest of the former: it is the poor and marginalized who, in the midst of their struggle, call upon biblical scholars for assistance in reading the Bible. This invitation brings together two very disparate sorts of readers: ordinary readers with no inkling of criticism who view the Bible as a text of life and scholarly readers steeped in criticism who approach the Bible as a text to be analyzed. The result should be an 'interface' in which both sets of readers do 'contextual Bible study'—a dialogue to which both groups bring their respective resources and in which both groups foreground their respective 'subject-positions', so that the power relations at work are always transparent. In this interface the poor and marginalized offer their insight based upon commitment to life, liberation and justice, with a call for similar engagement on the part of biblical scholars, while biblical scholars contribute their insight based upon commitment to criticism, with a call for similar engagement on the part of the poor and marginalized. Speaking-with is but another name for such interface and dialogue.

Third, such speaking-with makes radical demands on both sets of readers. First, given its point of departure in the realm of 'community consciousness', the concerns and aims of the community emerge as primary. Such consciousness calls for conversion on the part of biblical scholars—a conversion 'from below', involving social engagement and social transformation. Second, given its *modus operandi* in the realm of 'critical consciousness', the critical approach of the academy emerges as indispensable. Such consciousness calls for conversion on the part of the poor and marginalized—a conversion involving the self-conscious use of systematic and structured sets of questions in both the reading and the appropriation of the Bible. Thus, the poor and marginalized function as the driving force of contextual Bible study (by way of their commitment to life, liberation and justice), while biblical scholars function as its 'facilitators' (by way of their commitment to criticism). Consequently, the role of the scholar is not to bring a voice to the silence of the poor and marginalized, for such a voice already exists, but rather to submit to such a voice and to help bring it to full and effective articulation, since such a voice is but incipient and unstructured and remains largely hidden as well. In so doing, as West puts it, the scholar gives shape to 'counterideologies, resisting readings, and theologies that bring liberation and life' (1996: 33).

The actual mechanics involved in this process may be readily summarized. Both sets of readers participate fully in the process, although each set has different tasks. On the one hand, the poor and marginalized always determine the theme for the contextual study, usually choose the texts to be read, although the facilitators may be asked to suggest other texts as well, and always provide, in the light of their concerns and aims, the basic entry into the text. On the other hand, biblical scholars push for a close reading of the texts in question, provide—when called upon—historical and sociological information regarding the world behind the text, and assist in summarizing and systematizing the emerging reading of the community.

Finally, the intended results of such speaking-with is that both the poor and marginalized and biblical scholars read with one another, foregrounding their respective subjectivities and positionalities and hence the power relations operative in any such interface, and work together toward a proper and effective articulation of the struggle for full life, full liberation and full justice. Neither set of readers overwhelms the other; rather, each set becomes, in the process, partially constituted by the subject-position of the other, with both sets turning to the Bible in critical fashion for meaning and hope in the struggle, whether in South Africa or elsewhere.

Reading-with breaks with scientific criticism by way of opposition—it is the counterface of modernism. Although the competitive strain does disappear, it is a strategy that remains just as empiricist, objectivist and hierarchical. The difference lies in the hierarchy of reading posited: there is a reading for liberation and a reading for oppression. The Bible itself presents the God of Life and stands for liberation and justice. However, a liberationist reading of the Bible is possible only from the perspective of the poor and marginalized and thus demands the conversion of those who read from the dominant perspective, including biblical scholars. For the latter, this conversion involves the denial of the traditional claim to 'uninterested' reading, via submission to the concerns and aims of the poor and marginalized (social engagement for social transformation), but preserves the sense of criticism, which becomes its primary contribution to the liberationist reading. Within such a framework, the basic attitude toward the Bible is best characterized in the same terms of 'reading-with': the Bible emerges as the locus of the God of Life, but only in terms of reading-with those most in need of life.

*Androcritical Reading: Daniel Patte*
The second proposal, from Daniel Patte of Vanderbilt University, falls within the framework of poststructuralism—a semio-literary hermeneutics with a focus on texts, on the multiplicity of meaning-producing dimensions of texts and hence their polysemy, and on critical readings of texts.[7] The proposal is set against the background of 'male European-American critical exegeses' and described as a radical transformation of such practices in the light of challenges from a broad variety of fronts. Again, to understand its wherefore and élan, a grasp of its proposed context is in order, drawn almost exclusively in academic terms.

   For Patte, the challenges in question—arising from any number of 'advocacy groups' to the effect that the critical exegeses of male European Americans (by which he means individuals of North Atlantic origins and cultures, hence Europeans as well as Euro-Americans) are both androcentric and Eurocentric and hence patriarchal and colonial—are, though quite shocking and painful, entirely justified. The fundamental problem, however, lies not with the origins of such practices but with the nature of their claims. To be sure, such exegeses, as the use of the plural indicates, are by no means uniform and stable but rather diverse and in flux, owing to such factors as the diversity of methods at work, the heterogeneous character of the group, and the shifting nature of its concerns and interests. Yet all such practices have uniformly failed to acknowledge their contextual and interested character under the shield of critical objectivity, if not in individual terms (given the admission of presuppositions) then certainly in collective terms

   7.   I am relying here on what I believe to be his first elaboration of andro-critical exegesis (1995a) and its immediate expansion (1995b). For further elaboration, a couple of other works are helpful (1992, 1993).

(arguing for the complementarity of the critical enterprise). In contrast, Patte argues, such exegeses do serve the concerns and interests of male European Americans, who as a group have controlled the discipline, exercising throughout the power of inclusion and exclusion via their definition of 'legitimate criticism'. In so doing, the group has universalized its perspective and findings and stands guilty of the charges against it. From a theological point of view, Patte adds, such a stance is tantamout to idolatry.

The solution lies, therefore, in the adoption of an 'androcritical' perspective—the very opposite of 'androcentric' and 'Eurocentric'—whose fundamental point of departure lies in the acknowledgment by the group that all of its exegetical practices are contextual and interested, seeking 'to meet needs, concerns, and interests of male European-Americans' (Patte 1995a: 38). This perspective involves certain defining features: the driving agenda of the group; the rationale for and the mechanics of androcritical reading; the intended results of such reading.

To begin with, the concerns and interests of the group are defined in terms of a threefold commitment: to criticism, versus 'obscurantism'; to religion, versus 'secularization'; and to ecumenism, versus 'sectarianism'. This agenda is quite valid and legitimate but needs to be affirmed. Such affirmation has consequences. On the one hand, it calls for a view of the group's critical practices as contextual and interested, calling into question thereby any sort of claim to universality. On the other hand, it calls for a 'speaking with others' in dialogical relationship, affirming thereby the legitimacy and validity of their 'otherness'. Thus, in surfacing and embracing its driving agenda, the group posits itself as one among others, just as contextual and interested.

Second, such transformation in self-conception demands a corresponding transformation in interpretation: away from unidimensional reading, with its given search for *the* single and true meaning of the text, whether individually or collectively conceived, toward multidimensional reading, with a view of the text as polysemic.[8] The rationale is clear: texts possess a plurality of coherent

8. This transformation is grounded in a theoretical model developed by Mieke Bal, ultimately grounded in a reading of Jürgen Habermas's 'social semiosis' in the light of the semiotics of A.J. Greimas. Its major tenets are as follows: the concerns and interests of an interpreter are actually those of a

semantic dimensions; such dimensions are differently activated by readers in the light of different concerns and interests, making all readings contextual and interested; such readings, even if conflicting or contradictory, are legitimate but not necessarily critical; critical readings are properly articulated in terms of method and theory and yield semantic coherence. The dynamics are just as clear: a multidimensional reading foregrounds the plurality of textual meaning by bringing together a variety of readings, analyzing how such readings activate different meaning-producing dimensions of the text by means of the method and theory employed, and surfacing the various concerns and interests at work behind such readings.

Finally, the intended result of androcritical reading is to render male European-American critical exegesis ethical. Such reading calls for accountability and responsibility among critics: acknowledging the advocatory character of the group's practices and raising the question of consequences with respect to their findings. Such reading also calls for a collapse of the traditional hierarchical distinction between critical and popular readings: acknowledging all readings as legitimate and as ultimately grounded in a faith interpretation. Such reading further calls for a view of the critic as facilitator, helping to turn popular readings into critical readings. Only then, Patte argues, will the grip of idolatry be released, as male European-American critics begin to see themselves as an advocacy group—contextual and interested, a theological group —with a faith interpretation that has become critical, along the lines of 'faith seeking understanding', and a dialogical group— engaged in speaking with other groups and as facilitators with popular readers.

Androcritical reading breaks with scientific reading by way of textual diffusion—it is the plural face of postmodernism via poststructuralism, though based in literary semiotics rather than on deconstruction or reader response. As strategy, it dispenses with

group; groups are social entities—first and foremost, they constitute a 'discourse space', but they may also become institutionalized; as discourse spaces, groups possess a common kind of discourse and abide by a certain 'discourse interpretation'; such interpretation embodies a 'morality of knowledge' or 'codes' through which the interest and concerns of the group are addressed and protected.

competitiveness and highly relaxes hierarchy, while adopting a far more complex version of empiricism and objectivism. The difference lies in its polysemic conception of texts: a plurality of readings is the result of the plurality of meaning-producing dimensions of texts, differently activated in terms of the methods and theories applied and the interests and concerns behind them. The Bible itself, indeed any text within it, gives rise, therefore, to a cornucopia of readings, all legitimate—whether in agreement, conflict or contradiction. A properly ethical reading is possible only if this plurality of textual dimensions and reading activations is emphasized and analyzed in the light of methods and theories applied and concerns and interests at work. Within such a framework, the basic attitude toward the Bible is best described as a reading-about: the Bible emerges as a locus of multifarious meanings, to be approached by the reading-about of such meanings, always and perforce in representative fashion.

*Dialogical Reading: Kwok Pui-lan*
The third proposal, from Kwok Pui-lan of the Episcopal Divinity School, belongs within the framework of postcolonialism—a geo-religious hermeneutics with a focus on the reading of the Bible in the non-Western world in general and the non-biblical world of Asia in particular, with special emphasis on China.[9] Once again, a proper understanding of the proposed context, drawn largely in socioreligious terms, is necessary in order to grasp its wherefore and élan.

This context is constructed in three stages. Kwok begins with a portrayal of the Western introduction of Christianity and the Bible into Asia and China. The result of the missions is summarized as follows: a view of the Bible as the revealed Word of God and sole repository of truth—a Western understanding of its scriptures as not only superior but also in opposition to all other scriptures and hence all other religions of Asia; a view of such truth as personal salvation from human sinfulness—a Western dualistic understanding of human nature and destiny, unknown to Asian cultures and unattentive to social realities; a conception of such truth in epistemological and metaphysical terms—a Western understanding of

9. I am using an early draft of the proposal (Kwok 1989) and its later expansion (Kwok 1995).

truth not at all in keeping with the Asian focus on pragmatics. In the light of such beginnings and such modus operandi, Kwok goes on to depict the fate of Christianity in Asia and China as one of failure by and large: from a numerical point of view, very much of a minority religion—less than one percent of the population of China; from a cultural point of view, a religion very much per-ceived as foreign and identified with Western imperialism. Given such origins and circumstances, Kwok concludes by raising the fundamental quandary for Chinese and Asian Christians: how to interpret the Bible and how to conceive of themselves as Chris-tians in a world that is non-biblical and non-Western but which is their world.

Following a long tradition of Asian-Christian attempts to come to terms with both components of their identity, Kwok proposes the strategy of dialogical imagination, grounded mostly on inter-pretive practices already at work among biblical scholars in Asia but also partly on the deconstructive, ideological and dialogical practices of Jacques Derrida, Michel Foucault and Mikhail Bakhtin, respectively. The dialogue in question—defined as 'mutuality, ac-tive listening, and openness to what the other has to say' (Kwok 1989: 30)—emerges as twofold: first, it involves bringing together in 'two-way traffic' the biblical story and the Asian story; second, it calls for a multireligious search for truth in the light of Asian reality, with Christianity as but one of the dialogue partners in question. Since such dialogue goes against the established ways of reading the Bible and of Christian identity in Asia, it is said to require a 'powerful' act of the imagination, as Asian Christians seek to bridge the temporal and spatial gap between the biblical and Asian stories, to create new horizons with and amid the other religious traditions of Asia, and, in so doing, to reconcile hereto-fore highly disparate elements of their own identity. The interpre-tive process envisioned may be readily unpacked in terms of three distinctive components: underlying rationale; the actual mechan-ics of reading; and its intended results.

With regard to rationale, Kwok argues for a fundamental recon-ceptualization of traditional claims about the Bible: sacrality—the Bible not as the sacred text of God but as a human construction of the sacred among others, subject to testing and reappropriation in other cultural contexts; canonicity—the Bible not as the closed collection of God's truth but as a collection signifying both the inclusion and the repression of truth, subject to expansion by way of other cultural traditions and religions; normativity—the Bible not as the locus of God's presence but as a 'talking Book', subject to multiple interpretations and evaluations in multiple cultural contexts.

In terms of mechanics, Kwok identifies two overall approaches for bringing together the stories of Asia and the Bible: calling upon Asian cultural and religious traditions (myths; legends; stories) by way of comparative analysis—an updated version of the traditional history-of-religions approach; using the social history of a people as the hermeneutical key to the biblical message—a different version of the liberationist focus on the continuity of the people of God. These are not presented by way of prescription but by way of example.

With regard to intended results, Kwok's aim is to decenter the received Christian tradition of the West and to empower other cultural traditions both with regard to the Christian claim to 'truth' and the interpretation of the Bible; as such, it is a strategy that applies both with respect to Christianity at large, as a religious tradition among others, and within Christianity itself, encompassing as it does a host of different groups and traditions. Its consequences are clear. To begin with, it makes it possible for Asian Christians to appropriate in full their identity as Asians, alongside other religions and scriptures, and as Christians reading the Bible in a non-biblical and non-Western world. In addition, it makes it possible for Asian-Christian women to appropriate their identity as women as well in the face of both Asian patriarchalism and Western feminism—this feminist dimension of the proposal is present at every step of the way and reinforces the postcolonial angle of the proposal throughout. Finally, it makes it possible for all Christian groups and traditions in the Third World to engage in biblical interpretation and theological construction from their respective contexts—this liberationist dimension of the proposal is similarly present and reinforcing throughout.

Only then, Kwok argues, can the traditional hierarchical model of truth imparted by the West, with its concept of one truth for all and its exclusivistic, homogenizing and coercive practices, be replaced by a dialogical model with a focus on inclusivity, multiplicity and public discourse. This envisioned state of affairs is crucial for Christianity, above all in the Third World—a world of material poverty and social oppression, a world still marked by domination and exploitation by the West. Christianity and the Bible must be engaged, therefore, from a multitude of perspectives and contexts with liberation in mind—a liberation conceived not along the traditional lines of socioeconomic criticism but rather in terms of a 'multiaxial framework of analysis' (1995: 39), with a focus on issues of race, gender and culture as well. Such engagement can only be done by way of critical dialogue and public discourse.

Dialogical imagination breaks with scientific reading by way of reader expansion—it is the plural face of postmodernism via postcolonialism, grounded in Asia. As strategy, it challenges not only competitiveness and hierarchy but also empiricism and objectivism. The difference lies in its cultural conception of reading: a multiplicity of readings is the result of a multiplicity of readers situated in different cultural contexts and subject to different cultural traditions. The Bible is subject, therefore, to a plethora of readings—whether in agreement, conflict or contradiction—which must be openly evaluated in terms of their consequences for other cultural traditions and readers, above all the disadvantaged and marginalized, in the light of a more inclusive and just vision of society. Within such a framework, the basic attitude toward the Bible can best be characterized in terms of 'reading-among': the Bible emerges as point of departure, a 'talking Book', for any number of readings, to be approached by reading-among them in public discourse.

## Comparing Strategies and Postures

The preceding exposition has highlighted the differences between these three proposals and scientific criticism in terms of reading strategies and textual postures. A summary of these differences will serve to highlight as well the distinctive positions of each proposal vis-à-vis the others.

*Strategy.* First, all three break with the competitive strain of scientific reading and emphasize instead, each in their own way, the need for dialogue—reading-with, by way of the poor and marginalized; androcritical reading, with all readers, including the marginalized and the popular; dialogical imagination, in two respects: on the one hand, for Asian Christians, with their own cultural traditions and other religious traditions; on the other, among the disadvantaged and marginalized Christians of the Third World.

Second, while reading-with thoroughly retains the hierarchical bias of scientific criticism, though in inverted fashion (privileging the reading of the poor and marginalized), the other two strategies do not: androcritical reading relaxes such bias by viewing all readings as interested and theological, though it continues to stress the need for all readings to be critical; dialogical imagination abandons it altogether by arguing for full inclusivity and multiplicity. Third, reading-with fully preserves as well the empiricist stance and objectivist gaze of scientific criticism, but the other two strategies do not: androcritical reading adopts a middle position—meaning is in the text, but in abundant richness, which richness is differently activated by different readers, depending on method and theory; dialogical imagination opts for a more radical stance—meaning results from the interaction between text and reader, with the diversity of readers yielding a diversity of meanings, depending on context, in itself highly fractured not only in terms of culture but also in terms of class, gender and race.

*Attitude.* All three proposals break with silence toward the text in different ways. Reading-with yields what is best characterized in the same terms of 'reading-with': as the locus of the God of life, the Bible is to be accessed by way of reading-with the poor and marginalized. Such reading-with yields life. Androcritical reading yields what I have called 'reading-about': as the locus of countless legitimate readings, the Bible is to be approached by as broad a reading-about of such meanings as possible. Such reading-about yields tolerance. Dialogical imagination yields what I have described as 'reading-among': as point of departure for different readers in different contexts, the Bible should be approached by way of reading-among such meanings in public discourse. Reading-among yields liberation, but, since liberation is understood as pluri- rather than unidimensional, it does require open dialogue among such liberationist readings.

Such differences among the various proposals ultimately reflect differences among their discursive matrices: oppositional modernism; postmodernism by way of poststructuralism (textually based); postmodernism by way of postcolonialism (reader based, non-Western). It remains now to situate my own proposal within this emerging spectrum.

*Strategy.* First, against competitiveness, intercultural reading posits a multiplicity of meaning as foundational and thus emphasizes dialogue as well—a dialogue involving texts, readings and readers of all sorts. This dialogue involves more than a focus on the poor and marginalized of reading-with, more than the comparative exposition of androcritical reading, and more than a focus on the marginalized and disadvantaged of the Third World of dialogical reading. Second, against hierarchism, it speaks of academic reading as one of several reading traditions—a tradition as positioned and interested as any other, both in terms of individual practitioners and scholarly formations. Such a position does not subordinate academic reading to the agenda of the poor and marginalized, as in reading-with; does not insist on the need for other traditions to become critical, as in androcritical reading; but does agree with the focus on inclusivity and diversity of dialogical reading. Third, against empiricism and objectivism, it argues for a view of all texts, all readings and all readers as aesthetic, strategic and political constructions—a stance that calls for analysis of and engagement with all such constructions. Such a stance does not see the Bible as the locus of the God of life, as in reading-with, or as a cornucopia of legitimate readings, as in androcritical reading, but does find itself in agreement with a view of the Bible as a point of departure for multiple readings on the part of different readers, as in dialogical imagination.

*Attitude.* Intercultural criticism yields what I have described as 'reading-across'—the engagement envisioned involves a process of questioning of texts, readings and readers at all levels of construction, but above all at the political level of location and agenda. This process, involving evaluation and critique, is undertaken with the fundamental question in mind of who stands to benefit and who stands to lose in any such construction. This question, in turn, is pursued from my own perspective of liberation: first, in terms of marginalized and oppressed groups in any one context; second, in terms of the subjugated, exploited and denigrated in the geopolitical context of imperialism and colonialism. As such, reading-across does not privilege any one particular perspective as key to the Bible, as in reading-with—the reading of the poor and marginalized is regarded as positioned and interested as any other. It also moves beyond a mere comparison of legitimate readings in terms of method, as in reading-about—all readings are to be evaluated and critiqued on a sustained and systematic basis. It does, however, agree with the goal of a public discourse involving a multiaxial sense of liberation, while emphasizing the need for questioning throughout and adding an explicit focus on geopolitical liberation.

In the end, intercultural criticism and reading-across emerge as closer to dialogical imagination and reading-among than to either reading-with or androcritical reading and reading-about. Again, the differences and similarities reflect the discursive matrices at work: intercultural criticism and reading-across reflect neither countermodernism nor poststructuralist postmodernism but, along the lines of Kwok, postcolonialist postmodernism. The differences with Kwok amount to variations within the same discursive framework: a broader view of the public discourse envisioned—a dialogue involving all readers, readings and texts; an intensive focus on the geopolitical dimension of liberation—the focus on imperial/colonial formations; and a greater stress on evaluation and critique throughout—a dialogue marked by sustained and systematic questioning of all constructions. Such variations account then for my choice of 'reading-across' as signifier: the dialogue envisioned must be quite comprehensive, quite incisive, and quite challenging—the sort of dialogue demanded by my diasporic hermeneutics of otherness and engagement.

## BIBLIOGRAPHY

Barton, John
1998      'Historical-critical Approaches', in John Barton (ed.), *The Cambridge Companion to Biblical Interpretation* (Cambridge: Cambridge University Press): 9-20.

Kwok, Pui-lan
   1992       'Discovering the Bible in the Non-Biblical World', in R.S. Sugirthara-
              jah (ed.), *Voices from the Margin: Interpreting the Bible in the Third World*
              (Maryknoll, NY: Orbis Books, 1991): 299-315.
   1995       *Discovering the Bible in the Non-Biblical World* (Maryknoll, NY: Orbis
              Books).
Patte, Daniel
   1993       'Textual Constraints, Ordinary Readings, and Critical Exegeses: An
              Androcritical Perspective', in R.C. Culley and R.B. Robinson (eds.),
              *Textual Determinacy: Part One* (Semeia, 62; Atlanta: Scholars Press):
              59-79.
   1995a      'Acknowledging the Contextual Character of Male, European-Ameri-
              can Critical Exegeses: An Androcritical Perspective', in F.F. Segovia
              and M.A. Tolbert (eds.), *Reading from This Place*. I. *Social Location and*
              *Biblical Interpretation in the United States* (Minneapolis: Fortress Press,
              1995): 35-55.
   1995b      *Ethics of Biblical Interpretation: A Reevaluation* (Louisville, KY: West-
              minster/John Knox Press, 1995).
Patte, Daniel, and Gary Phillips
   1992       'A Fundamental Condition for Ethical Accountability in the Teach-
              ing of the Bible by White Male Exegetes: Recovering and Claiming
              the Specificity of Our Perspective', *Scriptura* (Special Issue S9): 7-28.
Segovia, Fernando F.
   1995a      ' "And They Began to Speak in Other Tongues": Competing Modes
              of Discourse in Contemporary Biblical Criticism', in F.F. Segovia
              and M.A. Tolbert (eds.), *Reading from This Place*. I. *Social Location and*
              *Biblical Interpretation in the United States* (Minneapolis: Fortress Press):
              1-32.
   1995b      'Toward a Hermeneutics of the Diaspora: A Hermeneutics of Other-
              ness and Engagement', in F.F. Segovia and M.A. Tolbert (eds.), *Read-*
              *ing from This Place*. I. *Social Location and Biblical Interpretation in the*
              *United States* (Minneapolis: Fortress Press): 57-73.
   1995c      'Cultural Studies and Contemporary Biblical Criticism: Ideological
              Criticism as Mode of Discourse', in F.F. Segovia and M.A. Tolbert
              (eds.), *Reading from This Place*. II. *Social Location and Biblical Inter-*
              *pretation in the United States* (Minneapolis: Fortress Press): 1-17.
   1995d      'Toward Intercultural Criticism: A Reading Strategy from the Dias-
              pora', in F.F. Segovia and M.A. Tolbert (eds.), *Reading from This*
              *Place*. II. *Social Location and Biblical Interpretation in the United States*
              (Minneapolis: Fortress Press): 303-30.
   1998       'Biblical Criticism and Postcolonial Studies: Toward a Postcolonial
              Optic', in R.S. Sugirtharajah (ed.), *The Postcolonial Bible* (Bible and
              Postcolonialism, 1; Sheffield: Sheffield Academic Press): 49-65.
West, Gerald
   1995       *Biblical Hermeneutics of Liberation: Modes of Reading the Bible in South*
              *African Context* (Pietermaritzburg: Cluster; Maryknoll, NY: Orbis
              Books).

1996        'Reading the Bible Differently: Giving Shape to the Discourse of the
            Dominated', in G. West and M.W. Dube (eds.), *'Reading With': An
            Exploration of the Interface between Critical and Ordinary Readings of the
            Bible: African Overtures* (Semeia, 73; Atlanta: Scholars Press): 21-41.
1998        ' "Reading With": A Call for Change within Biblical Studies', Paper
            presented at the Biblical Hermeneutics Seminar of the 1998 Gen-
            eral Meeting of the Society for the Study of the New Testament in
            Copenhagen, Denmark.
1999        *The Academy of the Poor: Towards a Dialogical Reading of the Bible* (Shef-
            field: Sheffield Academic Press).

# My Hermeneutical Journey and Daily Journey into Hermeneutics: Meaning-Making and Biblical Interpretation in the North American Diaspora

OSVALDO D. VENA

Because this essay deals with my journey, it is necessarily autobiographical. I will be telling my story, but at the same time I will be bringing to full consciousness my hermeneutics and my pedagogy. That is, I will be trying to understand the processes that inform both my reading and my teaching of the Bible. It is very important that I clarify at the very beginning that what follows bears the marks of my own subjectivity. This piece reflects the way in which I experienced the gospel as it was communicated to me by a church that was founded by North American missionaries. I do not claim universality or that my reading is objective. I will claim that it is accurate, because it corresponds faithfully to the impact this religious ideology had on an individual from childhood to adulthood. This simple fact cannot be overemphasized and certainly should not be understated.

## About Text, Meaning and Liberation: A Personal Testimony

This is a journey that involves a text, a sacred text, and my relationship with it. This relationship began when I was six years old. My father, a cobbler who attended school only to third grade, taught me my first letters using an old 1912 Reina Valera version of the Spanish Bible. I learned how to read my first words in a sacred text. I knew I was reading from the Word of God. I was deciphering God's language, not human language. From the beginning my relationship with the text was based on this premise: the text was God's word. Everything in it had supreme value and relevance. It was to be preferred over any other book. It was 'the book', written by God, parts of it even with God's own finger.

*Life under the Tyranny of Strict Literalism: The Text Means What It Says*
My father converted from Roman Catholicism to Protestantism shortly before I was born. Therefore, I grew up in a home where the Bible played a central role. My denomination was very conservative. It had originated in the United States and had come to Argentina in the early years of this century. Its interpretation of the Bible was literal: the text means what it says. The task of the reader was to accept its self-evident truth. It was a matter of faith, not human reasoning. This was particularly true, and embarrassing, when it came to the Genesis account of creation. We were made to believe, scientific evidence to the contrary, that the universe was made in six days! I would debate for hours with my high school peers concerning the validity of the Bible's account and the wrongfulness of the scientific approach. The Bible was God's word and it was authoritative even on scientific and historical issues. Furthermore, even Joshua's command to stop the sun at midday was to be believed as factual. It really happened because the Bible said so. This is what Carl Holladay has called 'the Divine Oracle paradigm' (Holladay 1994: 126).

The missionaries taught us to use the Bible as a sort of hermeneutical tool with which to interpret society. Society only made sense if it could be named or understood in biblical terms. The language of the Bible became an important part of our daily vocabulary inside and outside the church. This biblical jargon made it very difficult for us, actually almost impossible, truly to communicate with those who did not share our symbolic universe. I completed my first theological degree holding tight to the assumptions described above.

*The Beginning of the End of the Enslavement to the Letter of the Text:*
*The Text Means What It Means (What the Original Authors Intended*
*It to Mean)*
During my second theological degree, which I pursued in the United States, things began to change, partly due to a few influential professors who dared to challenge my understanding of the biblical text. Still, the setting in which I engaged it was again traditional

and conservative. One of those professors once made a statement that changed the way I saw the Bible. He said, 'The Bible does not mean what it says. It means what it means.' He was saying that the meaning of the text was not self-evident. It had to be brought to the surface; it had to be mined. And how was this done? By carefully studying the original *Sitz im Leben* in order to understand the intention of the original author. Through text, source, form and redaction criticism we were guided in a fascinating journey into the world of the text. The results of my hermeneutical endeavors were still very traditional, because the assumptions of the interpreter were not disclosed, but at least I now had some tools that allowed me to visit the world of the text. I began to see the biblical writers as authors in their own right, with theological agendas that guided their work, even if these agendas were still those of the orthodox church.

During my study for a third theological degree, I deepened my understanding of the historical-critical methods. I learned to appreciate the author's selection of traditions, his creative work of redaction and composition, his particular theological twist and pastoral concern for the audience. Here it is important to notice my use of the masculine personal pronoun *he*. At this point in my seminary career, all the biblical authors were unquestionably *he*s.

It was during this time that I was introduced to some of the contextual theologies that were emerging: Latin American Liberation Theology, Feminist Theology and Black Theology. I became very interested in the way these theologies had developed reading the text in a different way. Since the issue of *social location* had not crossed my mind as yet, all these new readings and their methodologies were still suspect. I was not ready to accept that one could approach the text from different perspectives, all of them 'equally legitimate and potentially valid' (Patte 1995: 55).

*Halfway through the Wilderness: The Text Means More than What It Means (More than What the Original Authors Intended It to Mean)*
An important development took place when I was doing my doctorate. One of my professors introduced to me the idea of the text having a *surplus* or an *accumulation* of meaning (Croatto 1987: 35). This was truly revolutionary. The text was set free from the tyranny of the original author's intention and was allowed to have a life of

its own. The original setting and the original audience came to play a secondary role and the text as a self-contained literary piece was brought to the surface. This new approach to the biblical text still emphasized the presence of meaning *in* the text, not outside of it. The task of the interpreter was to access this surplus of meaning codified in the text using insights from the sciences of language, especially linguistics and narrative semiotics (p. 9).

This stage was very important because it authorized me to exercise my innate capacity for grammatical analysis and made the act of drawing conclusions a life-giving, fun part of the hermeneutical process. It was at this point, when I was consciously disagreeing with traditional scholars on the basis of my own creative work, that I found this method most liberating. I finally was able to have a say, to express my own opinion about the text. Sure enough, the text still set some limits to my agenda as interpreter, but I was finally able to find my own voice. Or so I thought. Another stage lay in store for me of which I was not yet aware.

*Free at Last! The Text Means What I Make It Mean (The Role of the Reader in the Production of Meaning)*
When I began to teach New Testament, one of my tasks was to catch up with the massive amount of literature that had been written during the time I had been unemployed. Among other methodologies I began to read about narrative criticism, reader response and deconstruction. The first of these, narrative criticism, was not new to me, since it shared many of the presuppositions of structuralism, especially the focus on the text itself (Struthers Malbon 1992: 26). But reader response and deconstruction introduced a new element: the role of the reader as a partner with the text in the production of meaning—the reader as co-producer of meaning. This boldly affirms that meaning does not reside solely in the text but is created by the interaction between text and reader in the temporal act of reading.

This concept was the last link to be cut in the chain that bound me to the text as the inerrant, revealed word of God. Now I was free to engage the text creatively, making use of all the potentialities inherent in me as an individual, but also being aware of the limitations imposed on me by my own social location. I became utterly aware of the existence of other readers doing the same

thing, but from their contexts. The words 'contextual', 'vernacu-
lar' and 'subjective' began to sound increasingly familiar and soon
they became an indispensable part of my vocabulary as an exegete.

By this time, I realized that my approach to the text had gone
full circle, from my original affirmation that the text means what
it says to this last affirmation that somehow the text means what *I*
make it mean. In order to be able to say this one has to acknowledge that the *I* doing the interpretation is being influenced by
a context. This *I* is never an isolated individual but a collective
*I*, because behind that individual always stands a *reading community*
(Massey 1994: 152). The reading community and the individual
that represents it are the source of the reality of any given interpretation. Apart from a community that reads it, the text is a dead
artifact from the past, incapable of having any life of its own. As
Stephen Bevans has said, 'The human person or human society,
culturally and historically bound as it is, is the source of reality,
not a supposed value—and culture-free objectivity "already out
there now real"' (1994: 2).

## About Cultural Estrangement:
## Living as an Island in my Own Culture

Because of my father's conversion to Protestantism in its more
evangelical form, we were as a family, and I was in particular, cut
off from the two main branches that connected us to our roots.
The first of these branches was my parents' culture. Both parents
came from a family of Sicilian immigrants who arrived in Argentina
during the early years of this century. They were practicing Roman
Catholics. My own parents had been baptized and married in the
Catholic Church and had their first six children baptized in this
church.

My father's conversion resembled the conversion of the jailer
of Acts 16: he came to the faith with all his household. We became
a Protestant family practically overnight. Because of that, we were
pretty much considered traitors, not only to the Roman Catholic
faith but also to the Sicilian and Argentine cultures. I grew up with
the feeling of not completely belonging to either Sicilian or Argentine culture. I was denied some of the most important rites of
passage precisely because they were grounded in Roman Catholi-

cism. In this way the second branch that connected me to my roots, my Argentine culture, was cut off from my experience. I lived as an island in my own culture, separated from mainstream society by virtue of my being Protestant.

*The Inculturation of the Missionaries: Schizophrenia ('in the world yet not of the world') and Cultural Alienation*
The only way to cope with this situation was to submit to the worldview of the missionary ideology. First, I was told that my existence in this world was temporary. I was only passing through. I therefore was to regard my life in this world as a non-event, a prelude to a higher level of existence in heaven. Second, because of all this my true allegiance was not to any specific culture. Culture was, after all, a human construct and as such sinful and doomed to destruction at the Parousia, which, I was assured, was going to happen shortly.

In the meantime, we were to live according to a sort of interim ethics symbolized by the Johannine expression 'in the world, yet not of the world'. Of course, 'the world' was represented by the institutions and practices of *our* culture. These we were supposed to avoid. On the other hand, other attitudes and activities were encouraged: hard work, punctuality, an obsessive compulsion to tell the truth under any circumstance, a goal and achievement orientation in life, defense of the concept of private property, and so forth. Only many years after this happened did I understand what was *really* taking place: under the guise of a Christian ethic we were being inculturated into the work ethic of North American culture!

I use the word 'schizophrenia' to describe this divided identity. Through a manipulative use of the Bible, and my subsequent feelings of guilt, I was alienated from my own culture and forced to adopt a different worldview. But I wanted and needed to be able to function in both worlds at the same time, and to a certain extent I did. I managed to make some very good friends outside the church. These friends were all Roman Catholic and remain among my best friends from the past. When I reflect about these events, I can see now how they helped me in the future to adapt to new cultures. Indirectly, involuntarily and certainly unconsciously, the seeds for crosscultural awareness were being sown during this time, but the process was extremely painful.

It was the sense of mission, however, instilled by the missionaries, that accounted for the biggest alienation from my culture. In the sixties and early seventies, people in Argentina were waiting expectantly for some sort of social change to occur. Because of a generalized unhappiness with the military governments that had plunged the country into economic and political chaos, some, not many, were putting their trust in the guerrilla movements as an option for a new society. The majority of the population, though, was hoping for the pacification of the country through a democratic process. In this context, all we evangelical Christians had to offer was the aggressive preaching of the need for individual salvation in order to go to heaven, avoiding the flames of hell (we actually used this language!). Our mission was to save as many people as possible from the deceitful attraction of political and social involvement that would surely lead a person astray from God and into a life of self-deception and eternal condemnation. With such a primitive cosmology, it is no wonder people laughed at us and considered us irrelevant and even dangerous for the future of the nation. Our opinion never counted. Whereas my Roman Catholic friends were active in political and human rights grass roots groups, we had neither political nor social standing. We were invisible.

*The Role of the Bible in the Cultural Captivity Imposed by the North*
The literal interpretation of the Bible to which I made reference earlier in this work proved to be a helpful instrument in this process of inculturation. First, it justified the deculturation, the stripping off of our national and family cultures by rendering all cultures sinful. Second, these cultures were replaced by an 'evangelical' culture, a true hybrid, a combination of biblical and North American fundamentalist cultures. We were given a new identity: *evangélicos*. Our national heroes were replaced by the heroes of the Bible, and now famous North American and European missionaries and ministers became our new role models. By equating the Canaanite and Greco-Roman cultures of the Bible with our own Argentine, Roman Catholic culture, the process of ideological validation of one culture over the other was masterfully accomplished.

We read the whole Bible as a 'Christian' document. This should not come as a surprise to the reader who will basically agree with this affirmation. After all, the canonization of the Bible as sacred Scripture brought into the same corpus both testaments as the patrimony of the Church. The consequence of this action was that in many Christian circles Jewish and Christian culture became synonymous. For example, when David killed Goliath it was by the power of God, the same God who acted through Jesus of Nazareth, the same God whom we worshiped. Furthermore, when Israel took control of the Sinai Peninsula, the Gaza Strip, the West Bank and the Golan Heights during the Six Day War of 1967, we all celebrated it as the victory of God's people. Moshe Dayan became an instant hero in the biblical sense of the term. God, our God, was behind the military operation, allowing Israel to recuperate the land that God had promised them in the Bible, our Bible.

At the same time, the guerrilla movements that had begun to operate in Latin America in the sixties, as well as some of their heroes (Ernesto 'Ché' Guevara, Camilo Torres, Fidel Castro), were considered demonic forces serving international communism. These movements, we were taught, were embarked on a campaign to overthrow the democratic governments of the continent with the intention of replacing them with atheistic, communist regimes like the one that had prevailed in Cuba.

Since any culture was deemed as sinful, Israel's victory was seen as a prelude to the end of the world, the coming of the Lord, the arrival of the New Jerusalem from heaven. In the last analysis Israel's achievements were important only because they prepared the way for the rebuilding of the Temple and, as we believed, the Parousia of Christ in connection with that event.

*The Impact of Missionary Propaganda on my Cultural Awareness*
I briefly mentioned above that one of the positive side effects of the missionary ideology was that it prepared me for future crosscultural experiences. First of all, it gave me a preliminary and unconscious taste of the North American culture. Second, it provided an ideological framework in response to which I learned to move in two different worldviews or cultures. The whole experience, however, was in itself a denial of true crosscultural dialogue

precisely because there was no dialogue! It was merely a survival technique that I developed independently of the intention of the ideology that had created these two separate worlds. The missionary propaganda would encourage us to go into the 'world' in order to rescue people, not to dialogue with them. There was nothing they could contribute to the conversation except an unconditional surrender to the power of the gospel. Ours was not a dialogue but a monologue, a preaching, an announcement of what was required to be saved.

The distinctive marks of colonialism cannot be glossed over here. It was a true conquest, a colonization of the mind and the soul, a rendering of the whole individual captive to a different worldview. Underneath all this religious agenda there lay another agenda, ever so pervasive and enslaving: the agenda of the neo-colonial powers of the North, who used the missionaries as powerful tools for the economic, political and cultural subjugation of Latin America.

My evaluation of the impact of the missionary work during the formative years of my life is that it deprived me from fully experiencing my own culture. I also think that this deprivation did not include all aspects of the culture but only those that would have hindered the paternalistic control that they exercised over our private and public lives. Unfortunately, the missionaries I came in contact with said little or nothing about the unevenness of gender relations in Argentine society. They actually benefited from it. The leadership in our churches was only male, and the few females who were visible were assigned female roles: pastor's wife, Sunday School teacher, and the like. Nothing was said about militarism and the violation of human rights by the armed forces and the police. We were supposed to obey the authorities because they had been established by God. It was only during the horrors of the dirty war of 1976–81 that some missionaries finally woke up to the sinful reality of thousands of *desaparecidos* (the 'disappeared'), a situation that they had been helping to perpetuate, if only in an unconscious way. This fact alone created generations of Argentines who later in life grew disenchanted with their religious upbringing and felt an increasing sense of guilt and identity loss.

## About Living in Another Culture without Completely Knowing my Own

Coming to live in the United States was an eye-opening experience. It was here that I became aware of my true roots, but this was not an instant occurrence. It took years. As I started the process of acculturation, I realized that I only had a theoretical knowledge of many aspects of my Argentine culture. I just had not 'lived' certain things, and this for the reasons I have outlined above.

*Fighting the Stereotypes: Hispanic Culture but Sicilian Ancestry*
In the United States I was soon given a label: Hispanic. I struggled with this because it was not what I would have chosen. Again, I felt that my life was being described for me without my consent by members of the Northern Hemisphere. What if I did not want to be called Hispanic? What if I preferred the label South American, or Argentine? The reason for this resistance toward the name was that in South America the term 'Hispanic' denotes somebody from Latin America who resides in the United States, especially someone from Central America or the Caribbean. I did not see myself as a 'resident'. I was a student and was certainly going back to my country where no one would call me 'Hispanic'.

In order to counteract this tendency of being identified as a Hispanic person, I began to search for a new self-understanding and this search brought about a new self-identity. People in the United States would point to the fact that since my grandparents had come from Sicily, that made me partly Sicilian. Aha! I thought, that also makes me European. So, strictly speaking, I am Sicilian by race and Hispanic by culture. That was an important development in my self-awareness, but for a time it had a negative repercussion. By making myself European I was siding with the dominant society and against the Hispanic people. Somehow it did not feel right. I did not want to be called Hispanic. That was true. But I did not want to be identified with the mainline Anglo culture either. The way out of this trap was the realization that as a Sicilian I was really not Italian but rather a 'southerner', a representative of a mixed population, a 'mestizo' if you please. Therefore I could relate with the Hispanics in their 'mestizidad' ('mixedness')

if not in their 'hispanidad' ('hispanicity'). The advantage of this
new self-awareness was that it was a name I gave myself, not what
others thought I was or should be.

*Coming to Terms with the 'Diaspora' Concept*
I always thought that the term 'diaspora' was meant to designate
people living in North American society who had been forced to
leave their countries of origin because of political or harsh economic circumstances. Essential to the definition of the term was
the idea of compulsory exodus. When I analyzed my own situation, I rationalized it by saying that no one forced me to leave my
culture. I could have stayed, but it was my decision to emigrate.
The truth is that the concept of 'diaspora' was not as strict as I
thought it was, nor was my coming to the United States as free-
willed as I wanted it to be.

   My first stay in the United States lasted six years, and it was due
to educational reasons: I came to study with the clear understanding that I was returning to my country after I had accomplished my academic goals. No one forced me to do this. I chose
it. The second time was different. The education I received in the
United States, and continued in Argentina during my doctorate,
was aimed at training professionals in the area of religion for
functioning in North American society. In my case, it meant working as a Bible professor in a college or seminary. These jobs are
scarce at best and nonexistent at worst in Latin America. My only
hope of finding such a job was to emigrate and look for it in the
social context that had created these positions in the first place. I
felt that I did not have a choice. I *had* to emigrate. My exile was
forced by my training.

   Contrary to the situation of many Hispanic people in the United States, I knew that I could go back anytime. I was not a political
exile. But that did not make the fact of the exile less real. I was,
for all practical purposes, stuck in a culture not my own perhaps
for the rest of my life. Like the letter that Jeremiah wrote to the
exiles in Babylon, I was to 'seek the welfare of the city' because 'in
its welfare you will find your welfare' (Jer. 29.7). A process of
assimilation, or better yet, acculturation was needed if I was to be
at peace with myself and my environment. This process of acculturation took me many years, but finally I was able to adapt to the

point of becoming fully bicultural, that is, developing a dual cultural personality in which the threat of confusion of identity has completely disappeared. I believe I have been able to develop what David Hoopes calls 'multiculturalism'. This is the state in which one has mastered the knowledge and developed the skills necessary to feel comfortable and communicate effectively with people of any culture encountered and in any situation involving a group of people of diverse cultural backgrounds (1979: 21).

*Recovery of Valid Cultural Elements from my Background for Hermeneutical Purposes: 'Mate' and Motherhood*
Having been freed from the cultural straightjacket imposed by the missionaries, I began to rediscover aspects of my own culture for hermeneutical purposes. It used to be that the Bible was used to subdue and neutralize our culture. The premise in operation was that culture was a human product and therefore sinful, not valid. The gospel had to be stripped of its cultural components in order to get to the objective core, its universal truth, God's timeless message for any individual in any context. What happens if we take the culture seriously, if we make the cultural components part of the message and not merely its wrapping?

Can we understand Jesus of Nazareth apart from the cultural categories that are used in the New Testament to describe him, such as messiah, Christ, savior, shepherd, and the like? The answer is no, we cannot. They are intricately united. God reveals God's Self only through the particulars of cultural contingency. Therefore, almost any cultural artifact in any culture can be used as a metaphor or an analogy to communicate some truth about God. Stephen Bevans talks about the sacramental nature of reality. He says that baptism, the eucharist, anointing with oil for healing, gestures of forgiveness, and so forth are concentrated ritual moments that point beyond themselves to the whole of life. He adds:

> They are moments that proclaim a deep faith in the fact that the world and its inhabitants and their deeds and events are holy, and that, at any time and in any place and through any person, these persons and things can become transparent and reveal their creator as actively and lovingly present to creation (1994: 8).

Here I realized for the second time that something in my life had gone full circle. This time it was my understanding of culture and its relationship to the biblical faith. What used to be evaluated as sinful had become an indispensable part of the hermeneutical process. With this premise in mind, and building upon Bevans's concept of the sacramental nature of reality, I searched my Argentine culture for elements that would help me convey some truth about the God of the Bible. I found at least two.

One such element is *mate* (mah'-tey), the national drink of my country. This is a type of tea made from the young leaves of an evergreen shrub of the holly family. To prepare it, the greenish herb is ground to the size of ordinary tea leaves. The leaves are steeped in very hot water in a hollowed gourd. The tea is then drunk from a small hole in the top through a metal straw called a *bombilla*. The straw has a filter to keep the leaves out of one's mouth. *Mate* is drunk socially, each person sipping through the same communal *bombilla*. We learn this practice from our parents and pass it on to our kids. It is both a beverage and a cultural sacrament. One author, at least, has recognized this sacramental aspect of drinking *mate* when he affirms

> when it is prepared properly, from fresh *yerba* of the best quality, and one's host pours water of just the right temperature into the mate, and a group of Argentine friends slowly, quietly sip the liquid through the communal *bombilla*, they are participating in an ancient ritual as calming and comforting as passing the peace pipe was for North American Indians (Fox 1990: 25).

Encouraged by many authors in the Third World who have utilized cultural elements in their postcolonial theological reflection, I began to put together some ideas around the sacramental nature of *mate* drinking. The following is but an example of the direction in which this kind of reflection could go:

a. In the diaspora, *mate* is a symbol of past events that have great significance for the individual. The drinking of this beverage evokes memories of family, friends and life's events, such as births, marriages, birthdays, funerals, baptisms, fiestas. By drinking again one enters into a kind of participative remembrance of the past, that in turns reminds the person of his or her primary identity. Like the Eucharist, it celebrates, as well as sustains, life. ('For as often as you eat this bread and drink this cup, you proclaim the Lord's death until he comes'.)

b. The sharing of *mate* symbolizes the sharing of oneself in the context of a broader community. The person who *ceba el mate*, that is, pours the hot water into the gourd, puts into his or her action all he or she is and offers it as a gift to the community. ('This is my body which is broken for you...this is my blood poured out for you'.)

c. The *mate* is sometimes defined as a companion. The solitary drinking of this tea acquires social significance, as the person is able to feel the invisible presence of other people dear to her and who at the moment, and for a variety of reasons, are not present. In times of forced solitude—such as separation from a spouse; the death of a relative; the loss of a job, of friends, imprisonment—the person feels *acompañada* (accompanied) by the mere drinking of this potion. The warm gourd warms the hands, and as the rich, bitter tea warms you from the inside, your heart is warmed by the memories of loved ones. This has become for me one of the main sacramental functions of *mate* in the diaspora. ('Do this in remembrance of me.')

d. Many a person has declared the healing power of a *mate* at a time of need. The idea seems to be that while there is *yerba* (the *mate* leaves) and hot water, then there is hope. *Yerba* is very cheap. Anyone can afford it. It is very common to see homeless people counting among their meager possessions a *mate* and a *pava* (tea kettle) to heat the water. The *mate* becomes a symbol of hope, of possibilities, of new beginnings, of better days yet to come. ('Until that day when I drink it anew with you in my Father's kingdom'.)

A second element is the traditional role of women in my Argentine culture. The following are some thoughts that came together on the occasion of my mother's death. In the distant diaspora, and not being able to attend the funeral, memories of my childhood came back very vividly, and I wrote this:

> I have been struggling to make sense out of the metaphor of God as a Mother. Feminist theology, though methodologically correct and theologically sound, has not been able to convey this image in a way that I could emotionally own it. But my mother's death did it. Suddenly, the metaphor came alive when my mother died.
>
> We are framed between birth and death and God is there at the beginning and at the end. Somehow this became more real when I realized that this framing of life between birth and death was happening when my mother died. When I was born she and I struggled

for life. I was born with forceps. When she was dying, I was sick (sickness, for me, is always a kind of foretaste of death). We were again struggling together for life/health. I made it through. She did not. But somehow she made it through also. Through death she reached life, everlasting life.

I came to realize, after my mother died, that God's presence in my life is like my mother in the kitchen of my home. My mother was always there, waiting with a sweet *mate* for me. God is always near, waiting, inviting us to fellowship with Her through the sharing of the bread and the wine. Mom did not do much talking. She would sing. I knew she was there because of the singing. God does not talk much either. But she sings. She sings songs of love, forgiveness, justice, songs of acceptance, songs of welcoming…

Mom's main purpose in the kitchen was to prepare the family's food. I remember being at the kitchen table, studying, and watching my mother prepare the meals. God prepares meals too. 'You prepare a table before me in the presence of my enemies…' says Psalm 23.5a. It symbolizes God's provision and protection.

Mom checked my homework. And God checks our homework too. She is interested in knowing how we are doing in life. And when we are failing a course or two, She will have a couple of suggestions as to how we could improve our performance.

Finally, my mother would tuck me in every night in my bed and in the cold nights of the Argentine winter she would bring a hot water bottle, a *bolsita de agua caliente*, to warm my feet. When my final days come, and I lie in my bed not to get up again, I know that God, my Mother, will come to tuck me in and She will bring the hot water bottle to warm my feet eternally. And when I reach the other side, I know that my mother will be waiting for me in the heavenly kitchen with a *mate* to warm my days forever.

In this short piece God is presented, first of all, as a female, as a mother, doing some of the things women have done in my culture for centuries. God is depicted as doing what no man would have done: preparing food, supervising homework, putting kids to bed. This picture of God is destabilizing when you consider that missionaries usually presented God as the conqueror, the victor, the almighty 'Father'. Instead, here God is in the kitchen, which in my culture has always been the domain of women. Rather than approving the role of women as circumscribed only to the kitchen, this metaphor depicts God as entering the realm of women and elevating it to the status of revealing the divinity. The beauty of the metaphor of God as a mother, and its powerful emotional connection with every person in any culture, remains still largely un-explored, unaccepted, and even prohibited in many churches in Latin America, churches whose theology and hermeneutical prin-ciples are still being dictated by the conservative North.

## About Teaching in the North American Diaspora: 'Now You See Me, Now You Don't'

Many a student in my classes has had this feeling of not being able to pin down my theology. To many I am a sort of theological chameleon, changing my answers when the question is posed in a different way or from a different angle. I have to confess that this makes me a little bit uncomfortable, but I recognize that there is some truth in it. If I am going to accept the role of context in hermeneutics, then I have to be ready to concede that our subjec-tivity, and the context that feeds it, changes many times during our lifetime. As the context changes, so does the meaning of the text for that specific situation.

Perhaps a better example would be that of jazz. The jazz musi-cian improvises on a melody that is well known to both the musi-cian and the audience. It is precisely this mutual acknowledgment of the 'official' melody that makes the act of improvisation more meaningful. The audience can follow the artist's musical explo-rations because they know the basic tune. Despite this basic fact, each interpretation is considered a new piece. It is 'the signature, the mark of identity, the face of a person in sound' (Rothenberg 1996: 9).

*Coming to Terms with All of My Hermeneutical Approaches:*
*Peeling the Onion*
I like to think that every new way of looking at Scripture builds upon the previous ones and that there is some continuity among all of them. For example, the text remains the same and the per-son who reads it is the same, although this person has probably gone through many life situations that have changed fundamen-tally the way he or she thinks and sees life. However, it is precisely the way in which we look at these religious ideas from many differ-ent social locations that changes the meaning of the text. As Brian Blount puts it: 'Because we also know that the human circumstance

is constantly changing, we can conclude that text interpretation will remain fluid' (1995: 184).

When we arrive at a new understanding of Scripture, it is imperative to remember that this new stage does not necessarily annul the previous ones. It is just another link in the chain of possible hermeneutical approaches allowed by the text when read from changing social locations. In order to have the whole picture, the whole chain if you please, we have to take into account all the links and recognize that the text allows for a multiplicity of interpretations that produce different meanings. When I realize this, then my previous interpretations are seen in a different light. I start seeing them as necessary stages to where I am now. Even though emotionally I might not feel that these stages were necessary, hermeneutically speaking they were. Why so? Because they represent my journey, my different social locations through life and how they affected the production of meaning.

In my New Testament classes I always find students who are going through some of my previous stages of biblical awareness. Here is when my history with the text comes in handy. As a way of identifying with my students, I try to revisit my previous approaches—from the colonial discourse of the missionaries, to the historical-critical methods of my seminary days, to th structuralist hermeneutics of some of my Liberation Theology professors during my doctorate, ending with the postmodern theories that I encountered when I began my teaching career. What I have found is that these methodologies have accumulated in layers that I peel off in any given situation in order to access the students' particular contexts. Rather than discarding the language of all these approaches, I find myself using them in different contexts (church, seminary) and in different ways (lectures, group discussions, private conversations) as points of entry into the students' own hermeneutical awareness in order to help them move on to new and uncharted territory.

*The Validation of the Students' Present Hermeneutical Awareness:*
*The Journey Continues*
One way in which I allow the student's journey to continue is to validate their present stage. This I do in many ways. One is to incorporate into my lectures their language and theological cate-

gories. For example, in one of my classes I distributed a handout that I entitled 'A Trinitarian Approach to Hermeneutics', in which I included insights from some students' papers. I did this in response to what I perceived to be a generalized concern with the language that I was using in the class. In this handout I acknowledge the role the Spirit of God plays in the interpretive process, even though sometimes the language we use tends to conceal it. I then go on to propose an approach that would take seriously each person of the Trinity in the hermeneutical task. I conclude the handout by saying

> The above described approach to hermeneutics does not nullify the human creativity but rather explains it within a Christian framework. We acknowledge that as we create new meaning for ourselves and our communities we are being empowered by the Holy Spirit of God to do so.

The usefulness of such an approach is that it utilizes traditional, familiar language to express concepts that are not traditional. It is better to say that we co-create new meanings through the agency of the Holy Spirit than to say there is only one meaning that the Holy Spirit communicated once and for all in the past and that this meaning has become normative for all the generations to follow. This makes the text an alien artifact—it does not belong to us—and the Holy Spirit an outdated influence incapable of being present today in new and creative ways.

The fear and threat of new language are also taken away. This approach starts where the student is and builds progressively upon it. As they feel comfortable, the students will slowly venture into the use of new language. This is encouraged but not required. By allowing students to use their own hermeneutic language we bring to the surface, and into practice, the different social locations in the class. When properly facilitated, this can enhance the learning process. We learn that our interpretations of the text are partial and that 'the full spectrum of meaning available in a text can only be appreciated by allowing a multitude of communal interpretations to engage each other' (Blount 1995: 178).

Slowly but surely, though, some students begin to change their social location. Sometimes after a few months they come to terms with their new location as 'seminary students'. This, as one might expect, has decisive consequences for their theological language. With their newly acquired language and social location, students then are able to engage the text from a different point of entry. But not everyone journeys at the same pace. The idea is to allow, to facilitate, the journey, but never to dictate its particular development in each individual. Our task as teachers is to serve as midwives. We are there to help deliver the baby, not to induce a premature birth.

*Changing Social Locations and Changing Hermeneutical Awareness:*
*A Multifaceted Approach*
The classroom is a wonderful opportunity to come to terms with the different social locations from which people come to seminary. One finds there students from Asia, Africa, Latin America, the Caribbean and, occasionally, Europe. One also finds North American students from different parts of the country. All come with their cultures and subcultures, their denominational and religious upbringing, their sexual and political orientations, their lifelong traumas and happiness, and all come to learn about the biblical text. They form a wonderful mosaic of life situations. A professor can do two things with such wealth: ignore it or celebrate it. I have chosen to celebrate it and to make the mosaic an intricate part of the learning process on which we all are embarked.

They all come with some previous knowledge of the Bible. This previous understanding has been imparted by their home churches and by society in general, and it usually reflects 'a worldview characterized by notions of scientific objectivity, disinterested reason, universal and timeless truth, and a focus on the individual' (Tiffany and Ringe 1996: 211). This is true even of students who come from the Third World, which goes to prove how pervasive the ideology of the dominant white, male, Euro-American culture has been in our world. A few, though, come with an open mind, wanting to learn and welcoming change, but the majority walk into seminary hoping to find a confirmation for their beliefs and worldview. And here is where things begin to get interesting. Here is where a receptive, understanding even compassionate instructor can make a real difference.

Because I have been confronted so many times in my life with intolerant, one-sided biblical instruction, I decided early in my career that the way to teach the Bible was one of accepting a person's initial interpretation as a point of departure for further explorations. Respect for others' position has always been of superlative importance in my teaching. This holds true even when after an entire quarter of having exposed the students to new and provocative ideas, the person decides to remain unchanged.

The challenge is to divest the white, male, Euro-American ideology of its claims to universality and make it what it really is: another perspective. When this happens, this perspective becomes not only necessary but important in the dialogue among approaches to the biblical text. It is another piece in the mosaic, another voice in the choir.

The influence of the dominant Western culture has been so oppressive that it has created great animosity and resentment among members of other cultures and subcultures. This resentment cannot be overcome easily, and once students become aware of this pervasive influence they tend to react aggressively and dialogue is impeded. One example should clarify my point. When teaching a class on crosscultural interpretations of the New Testament, I thought it would be a good idea to bring all the approaches together to bear on one single passage and to do it in a round table kind of situation. We had represented the Latin American, Hispanic American, Asian American, African American, Native American, Feminist, Womanist, Mujerista and Euro-American perspectives. I was asked to play the role of the white, male, Euro-American scholar.

The session was videotaped. Very soon into the session I realized that what was meant to be a dialogue had become an open attack on the Eurocentric position. We could not go beyond this point. I, on the one hand, felt very uncomfortable playing a role I did not believe in anymore. The students, on the other hand, saw this as an opportunity to get out of their systems all the frustrations produced by the conservative, northern European scholarship. I realized that it is easier to talk about dialogue than to have it. Still, the need for listening to each other—not well exemplified in this session—is a priority. The result of this will be the production of meaning through crosscultural and crosstheological awareness.

*Teaching as Celebration of Theological and Hermeneutical Diversity: Anything Goes?*

How does my social location described in this article bear on the interpretive act so as to produce this crosscultural and crosstheological hermeneutics? By crosstheological hermeneutics I mean the production of meaning that is accomplished in dialogue with other theological positions. At best, this approach will consider all theological discourses as valid contextual responses to the biblical revelation. Therefore, when people interpret the Bible, they not only do so from their ethnically conditioned or gender-conditioned social location but also from their theologically conditioned social location. In other words, I come to the Bible with a theological perspective that has been shaped by some specific religious traditions in some specific contexts during my life and that comes as an a priori in any hermeneutic endeavor. It is present even before I open the Bible.

If I am open to this crosstheological dialogue, then I will not hold my theology to be normative, but I will think of it as another component of the theological dialogue. I will then be able to converse with people who come from very different traditions, knowing that their views will provide an aspect that is missing in mine and, vice versa, that my tradition will highlight aspects that are missing in theirs. This kind of dialogue should be possible in a time of ecumenical dialogue. Still, many times the shocking reality is its absence in academic and ecclesiastical circles.

Teaching as celebration of theological and hermeneutical *diversity* means giving priority to the expression of diversity. That should be the only normative component in the dialogue that goes on in the classroom. By upholding diversity we recognize the contextual nature of all truth and the ontological and epistemological value of context. We become aware of the ideology of the dominant culture, which sees itself as universal and tends to view diversity as a problem to be overcome either by negating it or by isolating and bracketing it. In this way 'the dominant culture is able to continue to presume universal status for its own context and to grant its readings privileged authority' (Tiffany and Ringe 1996: 212).

In my teaching I consciously try to debunk all normative readings of the biblical text and make an effort to allow each student to bring his or her own subjectivity to bear on the meaning of the text. In that sense yes, anything goes, as long as the two partici-pants in the meaning-producing activity are held in the highest esteem, that is, the biblical text and the individual interpreter as representative of his or her reading community.

## Conclusion

'Therefore every scribe who has been trained for the kingdom of heaven is like a householder who brings out of his treasure what is new and what is old' (Mt. 13.52).

I find myself doing precisely that in my seminary teaching in the North American diaspora. I reach into the deeper layers of my being in order to reach out to my students and their needs. I allow each and every layer of my theological journey to surface when being recalled by a specific demand in the classroom. I bring out what is new and what is old. Everything is usable, good; nothing is to be discarded. Everything is to be reinterpreted by and from my present context. I reach into the deeper layers of my being to find the real me. I go through many layers of inculturation and social-ization, good and bad theology. Finally, the person that emerges carries with him aspects of every one of these layers, a combina-tion of the new and the old, of yesterday and today. As I look back, I finally understand what all these years of journey have been. They have been training for the kingdom of heaven. In my case, part of that training has been to be able to adopt a multilayered approach to hermeneutics and to teaching that prepares the way for the hearing of all voices in the church and hopefully in the world.

### BIBLIOGRAPHY

Bevans, Stephen B.
    1994        *Models of Contextual Theology* (Maryknoll, NY: Orbis Books).
Blount, Brian
    1995        *Cultural Interpretation: Reorienting New Testament Criticism* (Minneapo-lis: Fortress Press).
Croatto, J. Severino
    1987        *Biblical Hermeneutics: Toward a Theory of Reading as the Production of Meaning* (Maryknoll, NY: Orbis Books).
Fox, Geoffrey
    1990        *The Land and People of Argentina* (New York: J.B. Lippincott).

Holladay, Carl
  1994          'Contemporary Methods of Reading the Bible', in Leander G. Keck
                *et al.* (eds.), *The New Interpreter's Bible*, I (Nashville: Abingdon Press):
                125-49.
Hoopes, David S.
  1979          'Intercultural Communication Concepts and the Psychology of Inter-
                cultural Experience', in Margaret D. Pusch (ed.), *Multicultural Edu-
                cation: A Cross Cultural Training Approach* (Chicago: Intercultural
                Press): 9-38.
Massey, James Earl
  1994          'Reading the Bible from Particular Social Locations: An Introduc-
                tion', in Leander G. Keck *et al.* (eds.), *The New Interpreter's Bible*, I
                (Nashville: Abingdon Press): 150-53.
Patte, Daniel
  1995          'Acknowledging the Contextual Character of Male, European-Ameri-
                can Critical Exegeses: An Androcritical Perspective', in F.F. Segovia
                and M.A. Tolbert (eds.), *Reading from This Place*. I. *Social Location and
                Biblical Interpretation in the United States* (Minneapolis: Fortress Press):
                35-55.
Rothenberg, David
  1996          'Spontaneous Effort: Improvisation and the Quest for Meaning',
                *Parabola: Myth, Tradition, and the Search for Meaning* 21.4 (November
                1996): 6-12.
Struthers Malbon, Elizabeth
  1992          'Narrative Criticism: How Does the Story Mean?', in J. Capel Ander-
                son and S.D. Moore (eds.), *Mark and Method: New Approaches in Bibli-
                cal Studies* (Minneapolis: Fortress Press): 23-49.
Tiffany, Frederick C, and Ringe, Sharon H.
  1996          *Biblical Interpretation: A Roadmap* (Nashville: Abingdon Press).

# Does Diaspora Identity Imply Some Sort of Universality? An Asian-American Reading of Galatians

SZE-KAR WAN

Diaspora hermeneutics has gained greater currency in recent years as part of the postcolonial reading of biblical texts. Two biblical scholars in particular, Daniel Boyarin and Fernando Segovia, have independently proposed hermeneutical theories that take diaspora existence as starting point. Both privilege their hybrid identity as a site of productivity and resistance. Both suggest reading strategies that take seriously their own ethnicity or cultural identity, leading to a hermeneutics that empowers their own cultural and ethnic groups. However, even if one grants that ethnocentricity is an ineluctable feature of exegesis, especially the exegesis of ancient texts—as I do—it is unclear if such a hermeneutical stance at the end occludes rather than promotes *intercultural* and *interethnic* dialogue between contemporary groups (Brett 1997). Although ethnocentric hermeneutics undeniably has internal coherence, does ethnocentrism prevent interpreters of diverse cultural and ethnic backgrounds from achieving crosscultural understanding of each other? Or are we simply left with the unhappy dilemma of each ethnic or cultural interpretation becoming self-contained and closed off to critiques from others across cultural and ethnic lines? If the latter, are we in danger of reducing all exegesis to ethnocentric proclamation and all interpretation to biased reading? I will argue that a diaspora hermeneutics actually implies some kind of universality whose mode of operation is dialogue and cooperation.

In this essay I will review the contributions of Boyarin and Segovia and suggest how an Asian-American modulation of their hermeneutical theories might avoid some of the pitfalls of narrow cultural essentialism and move us towards a more generous cross-cultural universalism. I will then advance a reading of Paul's letter to the Galatians from this perspective. I begin, however, by reviewing the notion of hybridity against which background diaspora hermeneutics has been framed.

## Does Hybridity Point to a Universal Discourse? From Postcolonialism to the Globalization of Cultures

Ever since the groundbreaking work of Rudolf Bultmann (1960), that reluctant postmodernist, interpreters of ancient texts have become attuned to the presuppositions in their exegesis. It is widely recognized that interpreters bring with them questions to the text that delimit the range of possible answers that can be wrung out of the text and determine the interpreters' agenda of enquiry (1960). Hans-Georg Gadamer formalized this insight into the general notion of pre-understanding (*Vorverständnis*), which in his schema forms an integral part of the interpreter's own horizon and is in turn informed by the effective history (*Wirkungsgeschichte*) that emanates from the text, a history in which the interpreter participates. Hence the possibility for understanding.

All this paves the way for privileging the cultural and ethnic starting points of the interpreter in postcolonial hermeneutics, a hermeneutics that could rightly be called *ethnocentric*. If the interpretation of an ancient text is to be a crosscultural exercise, the interpreter must bring the cultural background of the text into comparison with his or her own and, in so doing, unavoidably taint the interpretation, wittingly or unwittingly, with some kind of ethnocentrism. Either the interpreter attempts an *emic* description of the ancient text, that is, describing the text purely from the perspective of the original authors, going 'native' as it were (Geertz 1973)—assuming it is possible to do so—in which case no crosscultural understanding can be achieved. Or the interpreter makes an *etic* attempt to describe the text as 'Other', that is, to impose his or her own analytic categories of understanding or perception on the text in order to describe it in terms intelligible to his or her own cultural and ethnic settings, thereby inscribing, to however small a degree, his or her modern experience (Brett 1996: 6-7;

Craffert 1996; Eilberg-Schwartz 1990; Hoy 1991: 42; Taylor 1985; Yeo 1995: 42).

However, though ethnocentric interpretation might be inevitable, it does not necessarily lead to an ethnocentric *politics of identity*. In fact, as Etienne Balibar has demonstrated, the sort of anthropology championed by Claude Lévi-Strauss, according to which all cultures are equally valid and are therefore above criticism by any other culture, has unintentionally led to the xenophobic rhetorics of ultra-rightist groups in Europe and especially his home country France. If all cultural groupings have equal right to insular, separate existence, so goes the argument, immigrants and minorities groups deemed different from the dominant culture should also keep their distance (Balibar 1991a, 1991b). An originally anti-imperialistic strategy to protect minority rights by sealing off all possibilities of intercultural and crosscultural exchanges has ironically given fuel to political chauvinism. Ethnocentric hermeneutics, even with all its affirmation of identity and group solidarity—rightly in my view—all too easily gives way to cultural and ethnic self-aggrandizement and destructive essentialism. In the felicitous phrase of Homi Bhabha, without crosscultural and interethnic critiques, we are in danger of being seduced by 'the celebratory romance of the past' or by an attempt at 'homogenising the history of the present' (1994a: 9).

The alternative to ethnocentric insularity, however, is not a return to universalist pretension, which is often but the universalization of the dominant cultural values and hierarchy, but the notion of *hybridity*. Commenting on Frantz Fanon's *Black Skin, White Masks*, Bhabha suggests that the divide between Blacks and Whites—social constructs both—or between colonizers and colonized is not as clear-cut as one might think. It is, rather, a continuum framed between the extreme poles of the Colonialist Self and the Colonized Other; it is this in-between space where the vast expanse of hybrid existence obtains. Hybridity, in Bhabha's eloquent words, is

> a doubling, dissembling image of being in at least two places at once which makes it impossible for the devalued, insatiable evolué (an abandonment neurotic, Fanon claims) to accept the coloniser's invitation to identity: 'You're a doctor, a writer, a student, you're *different*, you're one of *us*'. It is precisely in that ambivalent use of 'different'—to be different from those that are different makes you the same—that the Unconscious speaks of the form of Otherness,

the tethered shadow of deferral and displacement. It is not the Colonialist Self or the Colonised Other, but the disturbing distance in between that constitutes the figure of colonial otherness—the White man's artifice inscribed on the Black man's body. It is in relation to this impossible object that emerges the liminal problem of colonial identity and its vicissitudes (1994b: 117).

If that is the case, this 'colonial identity', this ambivalent position of being 'in two places at once', characterizes all the colonized, and, if I understand Bhabha correctly, even the colonizers themselves. There are of course diverse modalities of hybridity, such as 'forced assimilation, internalized self-rejection, political co-operation, social conformism, cultural mimicry, and creative transcendence' (Shohat 1993: 110). Nevertheless, even granting that, Bhabha has to be credited with noting that the colonial discourse itself is not all-powerful (*pace* Edward Said) but rather inherently unstable, ambiguous, fractured. This is so because the colonial discourse is never transmitted perfectly to the natives but is always transformed by a process of translation, indigenization and contextualization. Bhabha notes, for example, how, in the dissemination of the Bible in India, the Bible is unfailingly hybridized and the received message indigenized. He writes, 'The colonial presence is always ambivalent, split between its appearance as original and authoritative and its articulation as repetition and difference' (1994c: 107). The gap left by this 'split' in colonial discourse is a site for resistance:

> Resistance is not necessarily an oppositional act of political intention, nor is it the simple negation or the exclusion of the 'content' of another culture, as difference once perceived...[but] the effect of an ambivalence produced within the rules of recognition of dominating discourses as they articulate the signs of cultural difference (1994c: 109).

Ultimately, colonial authority 'undermines itself by not being able to replicate its own self perfectly' (Loomba 1998: 177).

If hybridity is the common condition shared by both the colonizer and the colonized, even between 'one post*colonial* intellectual and another' (Dirlik 1994: 342), it seems to hold out the promise that it could be a kind of common ground for universal discourse between former colonizers and the colonized and between the colonized themselves. Caught in the painful throes of colonialism and its immediate aftermath, it is easy, indeed necessary, to retell the wretched story of colonization in conjunction with, and paving the way for, a national consciousness. However, as Fanon warns in his study of African culture, an unconditional affirmation of a particular culture merely reinstates the prejudices embodied in the unconditional affirmation of European culture (1990: 171), whereas wider and more expansive transnational solidarities between nations are more compelling than national cultures fixated on narrow nationalism. National consciousness ought to prepare for the emergence of an ethically and politically enlightened global community:

> The consciousness of the self is not the closing of a door to communication. Philosophic thought teaches us, on the contrary, that it is its guarantee. National consciousness, which is not nationalism, is the only thing that will give us an international dimension (1990: 199).

Said likewise adds that postcolonialism ought to facilitate the emergence of a 'postnationalism': 'Nativism is *not* the only alternative. There is the possibility of a more generous and pluralistic vision of the world' (1994: 277). In light of these considerations, 'Postcoloniality', Leela Gandhi concludes, 'is just another name for the globalisation of cultures and histories' (1998: 126). Colonialism in this new construct is therefore less a one-sided oppressive force of evil than a cooperative venture (Said 1994: 269). This insight points the way toward finally getting beyond vengeful sorrows and lamentations over our colonial histories, necessary and therapeutic as they have been in our coming to terms with our colonial past and present postcolonial identities, and toward entering a new forum of equality in which we participate as confident dialogic partners.

## Diaspora Identity and Hybridity:
## An Asian-American Modulation

What is said about hybridity applies a fortiori to the condition of diaspora existence. Those displaced from beyond their home borders have also learned to put on 'a doubling, dissembling image of being in at least two places at once'. However, without homogenizing the diverse cultural and ethnic backgrounds and universalizing one set of specificities over against all others, which is precisely the failed discourse of fragmentation that our colonial experience has taught us to avoid assiduously—the new discourse must learn to distinguish between diverse ethnicities and experiences, that is, to discern the multiplicity of diasporas (Segovia 1995: 60-61). The hermeneutical proposals of Segovia and Boyarin reviewed here, the former from a Hispanic-American and the latter from a Jewish-American perspective, are therefore mirrors holding up the relevant issues for consideration in the Asian-American diaspora and not meant to be materially definitive. The shared commonality in diasporic hybridity will form a bridge between these diasporas. In fact, as I will argue, such communicative bridges are almost required by an Asian-American hermeneutics.

*The Hermeneutics of Otherness and Engagement of Fernando Segovia*
For Segovia, diaspora existence means alienation, and it implies two qualities: otherness and engagement. The basic premise of his thought is contextualization. It begins with the observation that both text and readers are situated in historical particularity and participate in real, concrete sociopolitical locations. This means that the readers of texts are not modeled after an abstract, well-informed reader presupposed by traditional historical criticism, a reader that thinks and speaks in confident terms for all readers; rather, it assumes real 'flesh-and-blood' readers grounded in and informed by their social location as members of the diaspora, in other words, the *other* readers. Applied specifically to his own Hispanic-American experience, this epistemological framework for the pursuit of biblical criticism is referred to by Segovia as

> a hermeneutics of the diaspora, a Hispanic-American hermeneutics of otherness and engagement, whose fundamental purpose is to read the biblical text as an other—not to be overwhelmed or overriden, but acknowledged, respected, and engaged in its very otherness. It is a framework that is ultimately grounded in a theology of the diaspora (a Hispanic-American theology of otherness and mixture) and that gives rise to a specific methodological approach—the reading strategy of intercultural criticism (1995: 58-59).

What Segovia means by 'intercultural criticism', insofar as I can determine, has to do with the fact that *both* reader *and* text are viewed as an Other. Any understanding achieved thereby would have to bridge the cultural gap between reader and text. What is unclear to me is whether a hermeneutics of diaspora has room for dialogue across cultural and ethnic lines. The unique feature in Segovia's hermeneutics is his insistence that the text, like the reader, also has to be considered a 'culturally conditioned other':

> the text is to be regarded, like any contemporary social group, as a socially and culturally conditioned other… Rather than positing any type of direct or immediate entrance into the text, the hermeneutics of otherness and engagement argues for distantiation from it as a working desideratum, emphasizing thereby the historical and cultural remoteness of the text (1995: 68).

By the same token, the reader is culturally conditioned:

> Rather than seeking after impartiality or objectivity, presuming to universality, and claiming to read like anyone or everyone, the hermeneutics of otherness and engagement argues for a self-conscious exposition and analysis of the reader's strategy for reading, the theoretical foundations behind this strategy, and the social location underlying such a strategy (1995: 69).

Finally, it is by foregrounding the cultural conditionality of both text and reader that makes 'intercultural criticism' a possibility, indeed a desideratum. The encounter between these two worlds therefore takes place not between two disinterested or 'neutral' parties but as a result of 'an unavoidable filtering of the one world or entity by and through the other, of the text by and through the reader' (1995: 70).

It is clear that what Segovia wants to achieve is to privilege the reader in his or her own historical, cultural, ethnic, sociopolitical specificity in the reading of the text. Though the text and reader are both regarded as culturally other and both are determined by their own social, historical, cultural, temporary boundedness, there is really an asymmetrical relationship between the two. The reader has sole responsibility for constructing meaning out of his or her concerns and categories in the act of reading, while the text remains the object of investigation (1995: 68). Here Segovia's indebtedness to reader-response criticism is evident.

> In other words, even when attempting to understand the text as an other to us, historically and culturally removed, we ultimately play a major role in the construction of such otherness; thus, even when considering the text as a literary, rhetorical, and ideological product, we ultimately have a major hand in the very identification and

articulation of its literary structure and development, its rhetorical concerns and aims, its ideological thrust, and its relationship to its historical and cultural matrix (1995: 72).

This is one of the meanings of what Segovia calls 'engagement', namely, the reader's engagement with the text. Another meaning of 'engagement' has to do with the reader's interaction with other readers:

> in attempting to understand the text as an other to us, it is necessary to understand as well how the text has been interpreted by others, by readers in a variety of different historical situations and cultural frameworks. Such an understanding also demands critical engagement with these others—a thorough evaluation of reading strategies, theoretical orientation, social locations, as well as interpretive results, reception, and aftereffects; again, the goal of such engagement is none other than liberation itself (1995: 72).

But the question must be asked: What is the basis for engagement between readers from different cultural and ethnic backgrounds, when there is no common agenda or shared forum in which to negotiate differences arising from within the diverse diasporas? The notion of otherness is well developed, but is there a common language or basis for engagement? Segovia seems to be proposing the common agenda of liberation (1995: 72), but 'liberation' is a notoriously vague term, especially since one group's liberation could, under certain conditions, become another's oppression. One need look no further than post-colonial[1] Hong Kong. Survey after survey indicates that the majority of Hong Kong residents, if given a choice (which was never granted) would much rather remain British colonial subjects, with all that such continual colonial subjugation implies and entails, than return to be part of mainland China. This conscious embrace of a colonial identity, in spite of obvious—albeit attenuated—ethnic and cultural identification with China, raises new questions regarding the issue of *recolonization* (Ying 1997; Chow 1993). Furthermore, in the formation of the Hong Kong population, the vast majority of first-generation residents fled to the British colony from their native

---

1.   With other writers I am using the hyphenated form ('post-colonial') to indicate the situation after the departure of colonial power and the non-hyphenated form ('postcolonial') to refer to the hermeneutical construct based on such a condition.

China. As a result, Hong Kong citizens have always willingly coop-
erated with the colonial government, and the relationship between
the colonizers and the colonized is one of mutual dependence
and not of opposition. It would also be wrong to call this relationship 'complicit', since it was clear that, in the last days of the
colony, the real bosses of Hong Kong were not the British but
a Chinese plutocratic contingent, a condition which continues
today. This complex relationship virtually guarantees that there
would not be any unrest or need for liberation (Ying 1997: 65;
*pace* Wong 1997: 96-97).

In sum, I applaud Segovia's critique of any simplistic attempt
that seeks 'after impartiality or objectivity, presuming to universality, and claiming to read like anyone or everyone'. I furthermore
agree with the spirit of his statement:

> [The voice of otherness] sees a genuine exchange with otherness—
> the otherness both of the text and of other readers of the text—as
> impossible without a preliminary renunciation of presumed univer-
> sality and objectivity and a corresponding admission and acceptance
> of contextuality (1995: 67).

But without a common forum in which to negotiate a shared agenda and to foster the possibility of dialogue among children of diasporas, the possibility remains just that, a wished-for, deferred
dream that may or may not hold any promise of reality.

*The Diaspora Identity of Permanent Minority of Daniel Boyarin*
In Gal. 3.28 Paul says, 'There is no Jew or Greek, no slave or free,
no male and female, for you all are one in Christ Jesus'. This is the
very foundation, the very basis, for Christian universalism. It is this
great universalistic principle that has made Christianity a world
religion, and not just the religion of the West (*pace* Huntingdon
1996; Walzer 1991). Is this universalism expressed here so
innocuous? As Segovia has pointed out, any presumptive universalism is often the cloak under which one culture imposes its own
particularities upon another. This sort of suspicion deconstruction-
ists have taught us to raise, and, sure enough, Daniel Boyarin criticizes that Paul for precisely this point. Boyarin claims Paul, as a
first-century Hellenist, bought into the prevailing cultural norm
predicated on an essentialistic dualism between flesh and spirit.
The body does not entirely disappear in Paul's theological project,

according to Boyarin, but is decidedly subordinate to the universal Spirit:

> Paul was motivated by a Hellenistic desire for the One, which among other things produced an ideal of a universal human essence, beyond difference and hierarchy. This universal humanity, however, was predicated (and still is) on the dualism of the flesh and the spirit, such that while the body is particular, marked through practice as Jew or Greek, and through anatomy as male or female, the spirit is universal (Boyarin 1994: 7).

Ethnicity, like gender, is of course marked in the body: we are Jewish, Greek, African, Asian, Hispanic, male or female, by the appearance indicated through our body. Therefore, once we bought into the Hellenistic sharp distinction between body and spirit, which, according to Boyarin, Paul did, we could then relegate ethnic, as well as gender, distinction to the realm of the body but preserve universalism at the spiritual level. If that is the case, the inevitable result is an elimination of all cultural and ethnic particularities. Boyarin continues:

> While Paul's impulse toward the founding of a non-differentiated, non-hierarchical humanity was laudable in my opinion, many of its effects in terms of actual lives were not. In terms of ethnicity, his system required that all human cultural specificities—first and foremost, that of the Jews—be eradicated, whether or not the people in question were willing. Moreover, since of course, there is no such thing as cultural unspecificity, merging of all people into one common culture means ultimately (as it has meant in the history of European cultural imperialism) merging all people into the dominant culture (1994: 8).

According to Boyarin, Paul in Gal. 3.28 attempts to reduce all ethnic, cultural, social and gender differences to a kind of 'coercive sameness' (1994: 9, 156). By this Boyarin does not mean to say that Paul has eliminated all traces of Jewish customs and practices. In saying 'neither is circumcision anything or uncircumcision anything, but a new creation' (Gal. 6.15), Paul does not forbid circumcision but relegates it to the realm of ἀδιάφορον, a matter of indifference. Circumcision is no longer the make-or-break issue in the economy of the new peoplehood. This is precisely the point to which Boyarin objects: to assign as a matter of indifference the very thing that Judaism regards as the highest expression of obedience to God is ultimately to deny the Jewish right to exist as a separate group in this new universalism. Paul's tolerance belies an intolerance of the Jewish commitment that circumcision is not a matter of indifference (1994: 9-10).

We should not, however, lose sight of Boyarin's nuanced wrestling with Paul's universalism and particularity:

> This [criticism of Paul's formulation] does not, however, constitute an accusation of intolerance on the part of Paul. Paul's gospel was one of tolerance. I claim rather that tolerance itself is flawed—in Paul, as it is today. Its opposite—by which I do not mean intolerance but insistence on the special value of particularity—is equally flawed. The theme of [*A Radical Jew*] is that the claims of difference and the desire for universality are both—contradictorily—necessary; both are also equally problematic (1994: 10).

Boyarin's critique of Paul is, of course, intimately related to the history of Jewish experience in Europe—through the Inquisition to the Second World War. Boyarin is right to point out the tendency of the dominant culture to universalize its own cultural particularities—so much so that in the name of objectivity all other cultural experiences and expressions are flattened out of existence. However, is the valorization of cultural and ethnic specificities the answer? Can we afford to ignore what Paul is recommending here, even if we grant Boyarin's assumption that the Pauline vision of universalism is socially flawed? Can we insist on maintaining cultural specificities without falling into the trap of racism? Boyarin seems to think so. An insistence on 'differences', in fact, is a strategy for survival and must be distinguished from 'racism':

> Any claimed or ascribed essence has two directly opposed meanings depending simply on the politics of the given social situation. For people who are somehow part of a dominant group, any assertions of essence are ipso facto products and reproducers of the system of domination. For subaltern groups, however, essentialism is resistance, the insistence on the 'right' of the group to actually exist. Essence, as such, always makes an appeal to the body, to the 'real', the referential (1994: 241).

Using the Jewish experience as example, Boyarin argues that the creation of a diaspora existence—living as powerless minorities among other minority groups, all the while insisting on Jewish particularity, Jewish essentialism, even Jewish superiority—was the key to the survival of Jewish identity in the diaspora. Indeed, it was not just a matter of survival; according to Boyarin, it was the *key* to mixing with other cultural groups that insisted on their particularities and Jewish creativity. This Boyarin calls 'Diasporized identity', which entails a state of permanent powerlessness and which, according to him, is the only way to synthesize the Christian tendency towards a 'coercive universalism' and the Jewish tendency for contemptuous neglect for human solidarity (1994: 235, 257).

Nevertheless, once the powerless becomes powerful, Boyarin admits, as in the case of the establishment of the modern state of Israel, once the minority becomes the dominant group, once Jewish essentialism is backed up with an air force, such continual insistence on particularities and essentialism becomes the ideological basis for oppression. The policy of modern Israel towards the Palestinians, the Other, is of course one of the painful realities a Jewish intellectual like Boyarin has to reckon with, and I applaud his courage to confront it with integrity and honesty. Given these two ways of insisting on cultural peculiarities, Boyarin advocates a permanent giving up of power: diaspora identity means a state of *permanent* powerlessness.

### The Asian-American Diaspora

How should an Asian American respond to Boyarin's proposal, which is something akin to the Pauline principle of *kenosis*, self-emptying? At first glance, it seems to be an ideal model for existing as a minority in North America, for we are in a diaspora, displaced from our ancestral land, and participate in a multicultural experiment, which Boyarin endorses. However, is being in a 'permanent state of powerlessness' a possible solution for Asian Americans? Is this hermeneutical stance a helpful model for the Asian-American experience or, for that matter, for any minority groups in North America, especially in the academy?

First of all, let me say that the principle of *kenosis*, the self-emptying of power, is practicable *only if* we have something to empty of. It is silly, even illogical, to speak of becoming permanently powerless or perpetually landless when one has no power or land to begin with. I can well appreciate Boyarin's contrast between Jewish diaspora existence and the state of Israel, an insistence of particularities that has gone bad, but, with all due respect, diaspora Judaism had long established a power base in Western cultural and intellectual life. Even in the beginning of diaspora thinking, in the establishment of the Yavneh Academy by Yohanan ben Zakkai, he did so in his own land, among his own adherents. In other words, a diaspora identity presupposes the coalescence of a group identity first of all, and then the availability of power to the group once it is established. Then, and only then, does it make sense for the group to maintain its specificities while making no pretense to impulses of power.

These conditions are clearly not available to Asian Americans. Our experience in the theological academy tells a different story. Throughout the 1970s and 1980s, before we were stereotyped as 'whiz kids' or 'model minority' in the news media—I say 'stereotyped', because this kind of media attention concealed as much as revealed our identity—we had no choice but to learn the master's language and narrative before we were allowed a seat at the table. To have insisted on our Asian-American identity, to speak the Asian-American language—before there was any recognizable syntax with which to parse our speech—would have been professional suicide. There was simply no room in the academy to allow an Asian American to say what I am saying now, to give due respect to an Asian-American perspective on biblical studies. Now, however, after we have learned the language, we are all of a sudden told that it is the wrong language after all—a catch-22 situation postmodernism has created for us. Now that we have learned to speak and write like our white teachers, we are told we should develop and construct our own narratives, or, in Boyarin's terms, divest ourselves of power and the basis for that power, neither of which we have, even now. Well, not so fast. Give us a chance to consolidate our community, to create a place for ourselves in the academy, to have some power, if you will.[2] Once that is established, then and only then can we fully embrace Boyarin's suggestion that a diasporized identity can in fact be the key to communication with all other diasporized groups.

This problem is not unique to Asian-American biblical scholars but is replicated in the larger field of Asian-American studies. Scholars like Keith Osajima and Chalsa Loo have long recognized the obstacle to establishing Asian-American studies in the acade-

---

2.   Here the notion of 'cultural mimicry' is a helpful way of problematizing this Asian-American ambivalence (Bhabha 1994d: 85-92).

my. Located on the margins, such studies frequently face the danger of criticism and cuts and questions of academic credibility:

> The challenge of building Asian American studies requires that proponents develop a new field of inquiry in a context of institutional norms, values, and practices that are counter to and hostile toward those efforts. Asian American scholars, seeking to stabilize programs through their own advancement in the institution, often have had little choice but to accommodate to the standards set forth by academe. This has meant adhering to an ideal of scholarship defined by traditional disciplinary values, which includes an emphasis on publishing in 'prestigious' academic journals, and a priority on positivist research models (Osajima 1995: 26; see also Loo 1988).

Asian-American scholars are therefore rightly suspicious of any theory that appears apolitical and nihilistic, as extreme versions of postmodern theories can be. Relying on Nancy Hartsock, Osajima concludes, 'We should be suspicious of postmodern theories that abolish the subject at the very moment that women and other marginal groups are constituting themselves as empowered subjects' (Osajima 1995: 31).

By the same token, we should also be rightly suspicious of any theory that confines us, however unintentionally, to a perpetual state of marginality and prevents us from participating in the broader discourse where authority, legitimacy and recognition reside. Our ambivalence towards diaspora theory may paradoxically well be a result of our present state of diaspora existence. Our cultural mimicry, an indelible part of our hybrid identity, has invested for ourselves stakes in the larger discourse, and we are reluctant to pull them out before we can achieve what we need to achieve, namely 'to develop critical analysis of the Asian American experience, which calls for informed political action to eliminate oppressive conditions and practices' (Osajima 1995: 34).[3] For that to happen, Asian-American scholars, while critical of the modernist abuse of reason, nevertheless do not abandon reason but 'leaves open the possibility that a critical use of reason to interrogate oppressive facets of modernism can inform the development

---

3.  For an introduction to the ethos of Asian-American culture, see Lee (1996).

of a politics of change' (Osajima 1995: 33, following Smart 1992: 181).

In short, an Asian-American challenge to diaspora theory is a stress on the side of what Segovia calls *engagement*, though it is an engagement that presupposes group and ethnic solidarities. While the notion of otherness has been helpful in coalescing and rallying minority groups without voices, it would be the height of irony if, just as the prize is within our grasp, it dissolves into oblivion. If the notion of otherness degenerates into estrangement and finally into isolation, we are cut off from the intercultural dialogue that forms the core of legitimacy, power, and authority. It would be a struggle of futility if we finally make it to the table of decision only to find a total breakdown of all collective decision-making mechanisms, fragmentation and defensive aggression. In that case we are left with self-legitimacy and esoteric power, which turn out to be neither authority nor power. The Asian-American diaspora is therefore characterized simultaneously and paradoxically by a need for group solidarity and by the need for participation in power-sharing.

To formulate a more compelling basis for engagement, moreover, would help break through what Manning Marable has called 'racial chauvinism and inter-ethnic hatred' (1995: 332). As the 1992 Rodney King riot in Los Angeles has made abundantly clear, the incident was understood in terms of a black–white binarism: American society was unprepared for the fact that Asians, mainly Koreans, and Latinos were somehow swept into the vortex of violence. Caught in old racism and new hatred, Asian and Hispanic Americans were once again lost in identity politics, even as the conversation on race was heating up on the national stage. Thus challenges Marable:

> The ability to create a framework for multicultural democracy inter-group dialogue and interaction within and between the most progressive leaders, grassroots activists, intellectuals, and working people of these communities will determine the future of American society itself. Our ability to transcend racial chauvinism and inter-ethnic hatred and the old definitions of 'race' groups in the restructuring of this nation's economy and social order, will be the key in the construction of a nonracist democracy, transcending ancient walls of white violence, corporate power, and class privilege (1995: 332).

## Galatians as Diaspora Script

Boyarin argues that the plight that drove Paul to the Christian solution—in deliberate contradiction to the famous and influential thesis of E.P. Sanders that Paul proceeded from solution to plight—is born of a juxtaposition of Hellenistic universalism and Jewish particularity. The question that troubled Saul of Tarsus was, 'Why would a universal God desire and command that one people should circumcise the male members of the tribe and command food taboos that make it impossible for one people to join in table fellowship with all the rest of his children?' (Boyarin 1994: 39). In a blinding flash of insight, an apocalypse—so dramatizes Boyarin—Paul understood that the sect that he had been persecuting was right after all:

> The birth of Christ as a human being and a Jew, his death, and his resurrection as spiritual and universal was the model and the apocalypse of the transcendence of the physical and particular Torah for Jews alone by its spiritual and universal referent for all (1994: 39).

Boyarin's interpretation of Pauline anthropology suggests that Paul's solution was based on a Middle-Platonic separation between flesh and spirit, the literal and the allegorical, so that the fleshly existence of humanity is subsumed under the Universal Man and the ethnic Paul is absorbed into a non-differentiated being, with no gender or ethnic specificity. Its linchpin is a strategic reading of Gal. 3.28, but, as I shall argue below, such a reading of Paul might be based on a flawed reading of this formula. Once this misinterpretation is corrected, we can see that Paul in fact turns out to be rather ethnocentric. To understand Paul's view of ethnic dynamics in Galatians, we need to look at the wider context of Galatians. Two major features stand out: covenant and the peoplehood of God. Combined, these two elements help define for the Galatian converts a diaspora identity that turns out to be not an erasure of their Jewish or Hellenistic identity but a hybridization of both.

### A Landless Covenant?
Paul was of course a diaspora Jew, but we rarely take seriously his diaspora identity in our interpretation of his thinking. Once we do, though, we begin to notice how it has prompted him to trans-

form key Jewish concepts and symbols—chief among them the covenant, that very attribute of Jewish particularity and cultural superiority—in the service of his theological agenda. In this respect Paul joins his contemporary, Philo of Alexandria, in turning a culturally closed concept based on ancestral land and ethnic homogeneity into a subaltern identity based on promise, not genealogy or land (Elazar 1995: 26, 43). The result is the diasporized notion of a *landless* covenant.

Philo had already begun reckoning with the notion of a landless covenant. The original covenant that God established with Abraham in Genesis 15 consists of three important elements: nationhood, land, and blessings to all peoples. Of these three things, Philo retained all but land, transforming the last into 'Wisdom of God'. Paul makes a similar transformation of the ancient idea of covenant in Galatians: he retains the elements of peoplehood and blessing of all peoples but omits the reference to land. He clearly retains the Genesis 15 notion of blessings to 'all nations', τὰ ἔθνη, which he understands to be 'gentiles' (Gal. 3.6-9). This is after all the main polemical purpose of Galatians: Gentiles also share in the Abrahamic blessings promised in Scripture. He also places the emphasis on covenantal peoplehood as promised in Genesis: it is his purpose to make the Gentiles into a people of God,[4] so that they might be called 'the seed of Abraham' (3.29). Like Philo's diasporic appropriation of the covenant of Israel, an attachment to the land is nowhere to be found in Paul. This cannot be accidental given the great importance associated with the land in Palestinian Judaism and the equally important disassociation from it in diaspora Judaism. Here, then, decades before the Yavneh formulation of landless existence by the precursors of rabbinic Judaism, the central significance of diaspora existence for the ongoing life of the people of God was already fully recognized in Judaism outside the land.

In this light, Galatians should therefore be seen as a covenantal document describing the pedigree of the believers (continuity with the Abrahamic Covenant), the formation of the covenantal community (the presence of the eschatological Spirit in midst of

---

4. So Esler (1996), but I think his use of ἔθνος ('people') to describe the new people of God is misleading, because it gives the impression that all preexisting ethnic groups are subsumed under a new ethnic group.

the Galatians), and the fundamental character of the community (love). The ethical section of Galatians (5.2-6.10) is not an afterthought to its theology but should be seen as ethical stipulations that are a standard part of any covenantal document. According to Richard Hays (1987), the love ethics espoused here is precisely for the purpose of the formation of a new people. The glue that holds the Pauline covenant together is love. Later letters of Paul (esp. 1 and 2 Cor.) and the even later Deuteropauline letters (Colossians, Ephesians and the Pastorals) still have to define the internal structure of this covenant further, but the basic contours stay the same: there is a mutuality within the new covenantal community, so that the rights of each member are supported through love (e.g. Gal. 5.6; 1 Cor. 13).

This love is defined by Christ's self-emptying giving of himself (Phil. 2.6-11), so that love between members must also be characterized by the cross, the symbol of God's love to us through Christ (Gal. 2.20), the foundational event of the new covenantal people. Using himself as an example of a recipient of God's love through Christ, Paul says in Gal. 2.20, 'that which now I live in flesh I live in faith of the son of God, who loves me and gives himself up for me', which is used as a paradigm for the Galatians' own conversion experience in 3.1-5. As a result of this transformation, the new covenantal people is bound by love to each other: 'For in Christ Jesus, neither circumcision nor uncircumcision counts for anything, only faith through love works through' (Gal. 5.6). The Galatians, furthermore, are bidden to turn to Lev. 19.18, 'Love your neighbors as yourself'. Even though the Law is supposed to have lost currency in the new covenant, the new covenantal life is stipulated by love for each other. Instead of being governed by a law that binds the community members to predefined roles, new covenantal life is characterized by a freedom that relies on the members' love for each other. The former is marked by strictures that serve to limit damages, the latter is characterized by promise; the former absolutizes a static pattern, the latter highlights the importance of dynamic negotiation between members.

Reclaiming the Old Testament *hesed* ('covenantal mercy') structure and its legal stipulations while renewing the understanding of promise in light of the sacrificial love of Christ, Paul is able to collect these concepts under the paradoxical term 'the law of Christ'

(Gal. 6.2). It is paradoxical because Paul has just given up the Jewish Law and the formulation here conveys the superficial impression that Paul is merely replacing one set of casuistries for another. This cannot be further from the truth. The foundation upon which the law of Christ is built consists of the original promise of God to Abraham as well as covenantal love.

The actual ethical injunctions in Gal. 5.19-23 are no different from moral codes of Paul's day. Indeed, they cannot be, if the new covenantal community is to exist in society as a functioning member; the community must needs be bound by the same laws and the same ethical expectations as the rest of society. But these old injunctions and morals are now used in the pursuit of building the covenantal community of promise. Far from a legalistic use of law for the purpose of prevention, which stands in judgment of the guilty, the law of Christ is seen as an active agent that promotes relationship between members of the community. Thus, the opposite of misusing freedom for fleshly intends ('[Do not use] freedom as an opportunity for the flesh', Gal. 5.13a) is *not* a negative prohibition ('Do not do…') but rather a *positive* exhortation to build one another up ('But through love become slaves to each other', v. 13b). Likewise, after a standard moral discussion on flesh and spirit (5.16-26), the true sign of fulfilling the law of Christ turns out to be 'bearing one another's burden' (6.2a).

*Galatians 3.28 and the Politics of Identity*
If the foregoing is correct—that Paul uses, though with crucial modifications, the idea of covenant for the construal of the new people of God—it is at least a legitimate question to ask whether or not Paul actually reconfigures the polity of this new group along *Jewish* patterns. If the answer is affirmative, then it raises the possibility that not only his political configuration but also his *theological formulation* of the new humanity is Jewish. In other words, if we take Paul's diaspora identity as a Jewish Hellenist seriously and if his political metaphor is taken directly from Judaism, it becomes a real question to what extent the formulation 'You are all one in Christ Jesus' (Gal. 3.28d) retains cultural and ethnic—especially *Jewish*—particularities. Far from erasing all cultural and ethnic differences, as Boyarin has claimed, is Paul in fact forming a new community along *Jewish* lines? Could Paul be accused of subsuming all

differences under *Jewish* homogeneity? After all, Gentile converts
to this new faith thought they were joining Judaism, not an undif-
ferentiated, essentialist, allegorical Man!

It seems difficult to escape the conclusion that Paul was ethnocentric, in which case he was no better or worse than any other
interpreters of biblical texts at avoiding the ethnocentrism that
colors all hermeneutical enterprises. But Paul deconstructs this
ethnocentrism by relativizing his own prerogatives as a Jew in this
new community. He does not wish to erase ethnic differences, nor
does his later life illustrate such a blanket erasure of differences;
his continual ethnic claims in 2 Cor. 11.22 and Phil. 3.5-6, not to
mention Rom. 9.1-5; 11.1, would argue for the opposite. Neither
does Paul merely want to consign ethnic differences to matters of
indifference (ἀδιάφορον). It is more than a matter of indifference
to Paul, for ethnic differences in this case are a matter of power
and authority. Given the social dynamics of the Galatian community, therefore, it seems best to see in the formulation 'in Christ
there is no Jew or Greek' an attempt to erase the *power differential*
in the new discourse.

Paul goes even beyond the question of political power. If Paul is
concerned with rebuilding the Galatians as a people of God along
the line of Jewish covenant, then this new 'people' is reconfigured
not by erasing ethnic and cultural differences but by *combining these
differences into a hybrid existence*. In other words, 'You are all *one* in
Christ Jesus' implies a new identity for the Galatian community
that is a combination of *both* Jewish *and* Hellenistic traits. One
could accuse Paul for being more Jewish than is absolutely necessary in his formulation of that identity, but at least his theoretical
model is a hybridized one, an amalgam of two distinct varieties.
This new people does not simply take over the traits of the dominant group. If that were the case, Paul could have simply allowed
Jewish culture to define the characteristics of this new group, since
Jewish Christians were the dominant group. Rather, what I think
Paul is calling for in Galatians is for each cultural entity to give up
its claims to power—as Boyarin suggests—in the creation of this
new people, *without*, however, giving up its cultural specificities.

The novelty of the Pauline vision lies precisely in the possibility
that these different cultural groups could live with full acknowledgment of each other without each one forcing its own claims on

the others. But they could do so only if they maintained and retained their own cultural integrity. A paraphrase of Gal. 3.28 in light of a postcolonial Asian-American hermeneutics is—paradoxically—'You are *both* Jew and Greek, *both* free *and* slave, *both* male *and* female, for you are all one in Christ Jesus.' In this dialectic conception, universality is upheld, but it is universality that is predicated on, requires, and is erected on the foundation of cultural and ethnic particularities.

Boyarin is of course quite right in cautioning us that when we collapse all minority groups into the nondifferentiating realm of spirit in which all cultural particularities disappear, we are in mortal danger of being violently absorbed into the dominant culture. But true to the historical situation of the first century, *both* Jews and Christians were subaltern minority groups; in such a milieu the Pauline vision of universalism made perfect sense. Trouble came when Christianity became the dominant power of the Roman Empire three centuries later, when the formulation 'there is no Jew or Gentile' took an ominous turn towards oppression and erasure of Jewish particularities. Can the Pauline vision of universalism be realized again in the post-Holocaust age? Probably not literally as envisioned by Paul. The Jewish–Christian relationship has probably been poisoned once and for all, so much so that perhaps the only proper Jewish response is Boyarin's: Jewish insistence on their cultural and ethnic specificities as a form of resistance. But such Jewish hybridity also presupposes the existence of a common discourse, however it is construed, as well as implicitly demands general tolerance in a society characterized by multiculturalism. As such it calls for a formation of some firm basis for universality.

What Gal. 3.28 says to us, indeed to all minority groups without a place at the table, is that, in spite of our powerlessness, we do belong. This is the genius of Paul. In the context of the whole letter of Galatians, Gentile Christians were in danger of being overwhelmed by the Jewish Christians in the early church, and Paul was keenly concerned with including the Gentiles who did not have a place in the covenantal economy of old. Therefore, when Paul says 'There is no Jew or Greek', he is already asking for a self-emptying of power on the part of his Jewish compatriots.

## Conclusion

I have attempted to problematize the relationship between diaspora identity and universality from three different perspectives: a
theoretical consideration of the notion of hybridity in postcolonial discourse, my own Asian-American response to the diaspora
hermeneutics proposed by Fernando Segovia and Daniel Boyarin,
and Paul's own ethnic and cultural perspective as a Hellenistic
Jew. All three considerations point irresistibly to the need for some
kind of universality, some kind of forum in which differences and
cultural and ethnic particularities could be affirmed, insisted upon,
and openly negotiated, and in which all parties, all as equally
'Other', could maintain a healthy dialogue without threat and
without falling into warring factions and arrogant negligence. All
three lines of enquiry signal a need to complement our commitment to Otherness with a recognition of engagement, a need to
formulate a hermeneutics that does not privilege one pole over
the other but dialectically requires both. Diaspora identity implies
an ethics of universality: ethnic groups within a multicultural state
can continue to flourish only if it can guarantee a principle of
equal treatment for and between all groups. If not, the question of
unequal power will creep in to overthrow the careful balance thus
laboriously achieved (Brett 1997: 7-9).

The issue of universality is, admittedly, a modernist preoccupation, as Mark Brett makes clear. Nevertheless, in the diasporizing
identity formulated by Boyarin between 'the universalist preten-
sions of modernist ethics' and 'the ethnocentric modesty of postmodernism' actually stands an implicit yearning for negotiation
and dialogue:

> [There is] an inevitable conflict between the universalist pretensions
> of modernist ethics and the ethnocentric modesty of postmod-
> ernism. Boyarin's work adds an important qualification to this dilem-
> ma, however, since he only defends (polyphonic) ethnocentrism as
> a form of resistance, i.e., when it does not possess the machinery of
> state. Unless every people group is to have its own government, a
> scenario Boyarin rightly rejects, we are committed to multicultural
> states. And states, unless they are to replicate the imperialist struc-
> ture of centre and periphery, require a principle of equal treat-
> ment. The implied ethics of postcolonial studies cannot therefore

do without modernism, it would seem, even if the ethics of resistance are postmodern (Brett 1997: 9; see Yeo 1995: 42).

What standards, criteria or symbols might be used in the construction of this central forum is a question that cannot be readily answered at this point. Suffice to say that one need not go with Jürgen Habermas's razor-thin notion of 'rationality' in his reconstructed modernism before we begin with the construction. One could easily appeal to, for example, William Everett's symbol of 'federalism' or Richard Bernstein's 'constellation of conversation' for resources. In the globalizing world of today, it seems to me, even as we affirm our foreignness, our Otherness, our alienation, as well as our ethnic and cultural uniqueness, we can ill afford to ignore the common conversation into which our diaspora identity inexorably draws us.

## BIBLIOGRAPHY

Balibar, Etienne
1991a          'Is There a "Neo-Racism"?', in E. Balibar and I. Wallerstein (eds.), *Race, Nation, Class: Ambiguous Identities* (London: Verso): 17-28.
1991b          'Racism and Nationalism', in E. Balibar and I. Wallerstein (eds.), *Race, Nation, Class: Ambiguous Identities* (London: Verso): 37-67.
Bhabha, Homi
1994a          *The Location of Culture* (London: Routledge).
1994b          'Remembering Fanon: Self, Psyche and the Colonial Condition', in P. Williams and L. Chrisman (eds.), *Colonial Discourse and Postcolonial Theory: A Reader* (New York: Columbia University Press): 112-23.
1994c          'Signs Taken for Wonders: Questions of Ambivalence and Authority under a Tree Outside Delhi, May 1817', in Bhabha 1994a: 102-22.
1994d          'Of Mimicry and Man', in Bhabha 1994a: 85-92.
Boyarin, Daniel
1994           *A Radical Jew: Paul and the Politics of Identity* (Berkeley: University of California Press).
Brett, Mark G.
1996           'Interpreting Ethnicity: Method, Hermeneutics, Ethics', in M.G. Brett (ed.), *Ethnicity and the Bible* (Leiden: E.J. Brill): 3-22.
1997           'The Implied Ethics of Postcolonialism', *Jian Dao* 8: 1-13.
Bultmann, Rudolf
1960           'Is Exegesis without Presuppositions Possible?', in R. Bultmann, *Faith and Existence* (New York: Meridian): 289-96.

Chow, Rey
1993           *Writing Diaspora: Tactics of Intervention in Contemporary Cultural Studies* (Bloomington: Indiana University Press).

Craffert, Pieter F.
    1996            'On New Testament Interpretation and Ethnocentrism', in Brett
                    1996: 449-68.
Dirlik, Arif
    1994            'The Postcolonial Aura: Third World Criticism in the Age of Global
                    Capitalism', *Critical Inquiry* 20: 328-56.
Eilberg-Schwartz, Howard
    1990            *The Savage in Judaism: An Anthropology of Israelite Religion and Ancient
                    Judaism* (Bloomington: Indiana University Press).
Elazar, Daniel
    1995            *Covenant and Polity in Biblical Israel: Biblical Foundations and Jewish
                    Expressions* (Covenant Tradition in Politics, 1; New Brunswick: Trans-
                    action Books).
Esler, Philip F.
    1996            'Group Boundaries and Intergroup Conflict in Galatians: A New
                    Reading of Gal. 5.13–6.10', in Brett 1996: 215-40.
Fanon, Frantz
    1967            *Black Skin, White Masks* (trans. L. Markmann; New York: Grove
                    Press).
    1990            *The Wretched of the Earth* (trans. C. Farrington; Harmondsworth: Pen-
                    guin Books, 3rd edn).
Gandhi, Leela
    1998            *Postcolonial Theory: A Critical Introduction* (New York: Columbia Uni-
                    versity Press).
Geertz, Clifford
    1973            *The Interpretation of Cultures: Selected Essays* (New York: Basic Books).
Hays, Richard B.
    1987            'Christology and Ethics in Galatians: The Law of Christ', *Catholic Bib-
                    lical Quarterly* 49: 268-90.
Hoy, D.
    1991            'Is Hermeneutics Ethnocentric?', in D.R. Hiley *et al.* (eds.), *The Inter-
                    pretive Turn: Philosophy, Science, Culture* (Ithaca, NY: Cornell Univer-
                    sity Press): 155-75.
Huntington, Samuel P.
    1996            *The Clash of Civilizations and the Remaking of World Order* (New York:
                    Simon & Schuster).
Lee, Andrew
    1996            'History and Issues in Asian-American Interpretation'. Unpublished
                    manuscript.
Loo, Chalsa
    1988            'The "Middle-aging" of Asian American Studies', in G.Y. Okihiro *et
                    al.* (eds.), *Reflections on Shattered Windows: Promises and Prospects for
                    Asian American Studies* (Pullman, WA: Washington State University
                    Press): 145-60.
Loomba, Ania
    1998            *Colonialism/Postcolonialism* (New Critical Idiom; London: Routledge).
Marable, Manning
    1995            'Beyond Racial Identity Politics: Toward a Liberation Theory for

Multicultural Democracy', in Y.O. Okihiro *et al.* (eds.), *Privileging Positions: The Sites of Asian American Studies* (Pullman, WA: Washington State University Press): 315-33.

Osajima, Keith Hiroshi
1995                'Postmodernism and Asian American Studies: A Critical Appropriation', in G.Y. Okihiro *et al.* (eds.), *Privileging Positions: The Sites of Asian American Studies* (Pullman, WA: Washington State University Press): 21-35.

Said, Edward W.
1994                *Culture and Imperialism* (New York: Alfred A. Knopf).

Segovia, Fernando F.
1995                'Toward a Hermeneutics of the Diaspora: A Hermeneutics of Otherness and Engagement', in Fernando F. Segovia and M.A. Tolbert (eds.), *Reading from This Place.* I. *Social Location and Biblical Interpretation in the United States* (Minneapolis: Fortress Press): 57-73.

Shohat, Ella
1993                'Notes on the "Post-colonial"', *Social Text* 31–32: 99-113.

Smart, Barry
1992                *Modern Conditions, Postmodern Controversies* (London: Routledge).

Taylor, Charles
1985                'Understanding and Ethnocentricity', in *idem, Philosophy and the Human Sciences* (Philosophical Papers, 2; Cambridge: Cambridge University Press): 116-33.

Walzer, Michael
1991                'The Idea of Civil Society', *Dissent* 38(2): 293-304.

Wong, Wai-ching
1997                'Asian Theologians between East and West: A Postcolonial Self-understanding', *Jian Dao* 8: 89-102.

Yeo, Khiok-Khng
1995                *Rhetorical Interaction in I Corinthians 8 and 10: A Formal Analysis with Preliminary Suggestions for a Chinese, Cross-Cultural Hermeneutic* (Leiden: E.J. Brill).

Ying, Fuk-tsang
1997                'National Identification and Identity Crisis of the Hong Kong People', *Jian Dao* 8: 63-88.

# Part II

## READING FROM THE DIASPORA

# Hyphenating Joseph:
# A View of Genesis 39–41 from the Cuban Diaspora[1]

## Francisco García-Treto

## Introduction: Diasporic Reading

> For people like me, the truth always comes gift-wrapped in fancy
> paradox: that our exile has already ended, and that our exile will
> never end; that no exile is forever, and that there is no after-exile.
> Sometimes I revel in this doubleness, sometimes I revile it, but the
> doubleness is me: I am *yo* and you and *tú* and two (Pérez Firmat
> 1995: 269-70).

My reading of the Hebrew Bible, itself arguably a set of books
largely written by exiles and for exiles, is based on my own awareness of being part of the Cuban diaspora in the United States.
Other interpreters who share the same point of view have already
begun to define its character. Justo González, for example, describes the experience of Hispanic exiles in the United States by
means of the conceptual pair 'center/periphery' and characterizes exile as

> a life in which one is forced to revolve around a center that is not
> one's own, and that in many ways one does not wish to own. Exile is
> a dislocation of the center, with all the ambiguities and ambiva-
> lence of such dislocation (1996: 92).

Fernando Segovia, moreover, identifies the source of the 'am-
biguities and ambivalence' in the exiles' experience as also the
source of an overriding sense among exiles that all worlds are
social constructions, and thus the grounds for the construction of
our own identity. If, as Gustavo Pérez Firmat has memorably put

1. This article develops the ideas of a brief piece of mine (García-Treto
1996).

it, to be a Cuban-American in the United States is to live 'on the hyphen' (1994)[2]—that is, in two worlds at once and as 'other' in both—Segovia is right when he says,

> We know both worlds quite well from the inside and the outside, and this privileged knowledge of ours gives us a rather unique perspective: we know that both worlds, that all worlds, are constructions... We know what makes each world cohere and function; we can see what is good and bad in each world and choose accordingly; and we are able to offer an informed critique of each world —its vision, its values, its traditions (1995: 65).

Like Segovia, I prefer to use the term diaspora rather than exile as a descriptor, acknowledging in this also a debt to Ruth Behar, the Cuban-American anthropologist. Her usage of the term is meant to reflect both openness to the variability of the life experiences of Cubans in the United States and inclusiveness of Cubans still living in Cuba.

> By choosing diaspora [Behar says as she explains her choice of the word as part of a course title] I opt for undecidability, a refusal to submit to the tyranny of categories: Cubans outside Cuba are perhaps immigrants, perhaps exiles, perhaps both, perhaps neither, and Cubans inside Cuba are in certain ways perhaps more exiled in their *insile* than the so-called exiles themselves... Diaspora also counters the Cuban tendency toward exceptionalism and the arrogance of insularity, allowing us to place the Cuban counterpoint within a wider framework of twentieth-century unbound nations, borderizations, and deterritorializations (1996: 144-45).

Behar (as well as Pérez Firmat) makes explicit the conceptual parallel that exists in the minds of many Cubans between the Cuban and the Jewish diasporas[3] and adopts the ideal of a 'Diaspora culture and identity' put forward for the latter by Daniel Boyarin,[4] who claims that it

---

2.    Note that Pérez Firmat affirms the hyphen, 'In our case, the hyphen is not a minus sign but a plus, perhaps we should call ourselves "Cuban + Americans"' (1994: 16).

3.    Behar cites the recent work of David Rieff (1993). The title of Gustavo Pérez Firmat's book cited above, *Next Year in Cuba*, is an example of conscious appropriation of the discourse of the Jewish diaspora to refer to the Cuban experience.

4.    In her book Behar cites an article by Daniel Boyarin and Jonathan Boyarin (1993). See also Boyarin (1994: 228-60).

allows (and has historically allowed in the best circumstances, such as Muslim Spain), for a complex continuation of Jewish cultural creativity and identity at the same time that the same people participate fully in the common cultural life of their surroundings... Diasporic cultural identity teaches us that cultures are not preserved by being protected from 'mixing' but probably can only continue to exist as a product of such mixing (1994: 243).

## Joseph: A Diasporic Story and Reading

The second son that Asenath bore him he named Ephraim which means To be Fruitful and the way he explained that name was by saying that the Fear had made him fruitful in the land of his exile. It was a name with something of gladness in it like the name Manasseh, but the Black Land of his exile had become in many ways more home to him, in his heart, than the land of the desert and the hills and the black tents and the season—following herds which more and more came to seem to him like a friend he had abandoned, and so there was grief as well in the name of Ephraim (Buechner 1993: 253).

Like Jerusalem's diaspora in Babylonia, like Latin America's diaspora in the United States, Joseph found himself in Egypt as a result of an unwilled uprooting, ripped away from the center that had nurtured his childhood and youth by the action of his own brothers, and placed (in his case as a foreign slave and as a prisoner) in the most peripheral of positions in a new society. At the same time, as for many members of the diasporas of ancient Jerusalem or of contemporary Havana, Joseph's experience in the land of his exile is one of settlement, assimilation and success far surpassing mere survival. Joseph's transition from powerlessness at the margin to practically unlimited power at the very center of Egyptian society is the subject of Genesis 39–41, which, rather than seeing it simply as a 'digression' in the story of the family of Jacob (Coats 1983: 265), I prefer to view as a central turning point in the diasporic story that Joseph the exile typifies. I find these chapters illuminated in a special way when I approach them from the point of view of a member of the Cuban diaspora in the United States. Pérez Firmat analyzes the new exile's process of construction of a diasporic home—or 'adaptation to a new homeland'—as comprising three stages, which he characterizes in terms of (1) substitution, (2) destitution and (3) institution.

*Substitution Stage*

To the first stage, which 'consists of an effort to create substitutes or copies of the home culture' (Pérez Firmat 1994: 7), belongs, for example, the well-known phenomenon of the creation of a 'little Havana' in Miami, 'little' not because of size but because of its 'diminished status as a deficient or incomplete copy of the original' (p. 7). 'The substitutive impulse of newly arrived exiles makes them ignore the evidence of their senses,' says Pérez Firmat, who goes on to add, 'Because the reality of exile may be too costly to accept, the exile aspires to reproduce, rather than to recast, native traditions' (p. 7).

Midrashic interpretation of the Joseph story long ago perceived that the early stage of Joseph's sojourn in Egypt, particularly the time spent in Potiphar's house, can be seen as a substitutive stage, where Joseph replays both positive and negative traits of his former role in his father's house and where for a time he becomes just as much the favored 'star' of Potiphar's household as he had been in Jacob's. Just as Joseph had stood out from among his brothers in his former life in Canaan because of the prophetic dreams that he recklessly told them, thus earning their enmity, so now, at first as a junior slave in Potiphar's house, again tempts fate by performing minor miracles. So *Midrash Tanḥuma* comments on Gen. 39.3:

> 'The Lord made all that he did to prosper in his hand' (Gen. 39.3). Whenever Joseph served his master spiced wine, the master would ask, 'What have you poured me?' When Joseph replied, 'Spiced wine', the master would say, 'But I want bitter wine'—and it became bitter wine. When the master said, 'I want mulled wine', it became mulled. The same happened with water—indeed, with each and every thing, as is said, 'The Lord made all that he did to prosper in his hand' (Bialik and Ravnitzky 1992: 52).

*Genesis Rabbah* 86.5, also on Gen. 39.3, is another notable example, which Avivah Gottlieb Zornberg summarizes as follows:

> In the early days of his captivity in Potiphar's house, Joseph goes about repeating (whispering) the Torah which he had learned in his father's house. This is his strenuous attempt to 're-member' his identity and culture, to keep 'God with him.' Since small domestic miracles constantly happen to him...Potiphar assumes that he is

> muttering spells... Eventually...Potiphar does recognize the heroic
> subjectivity of Joseph as he strives to remember God, Torah and
> himself. But in the end, the midrash begins—as though this end to
> heroic memorizing were inevitable—Joseph forgot (1995: 274).

Both *Midrash Rabbah* and *Tanḥuma* ascribe to Joseph at this stage,
along with his great abilities and attractiveness, the same traits of
self-centeredness and pride that had once brought him to grief
with his brothers and that now bring upon him the events that are
to lead him again to grief. James Kugel, citing *Tanḥuma* and the
*Testament of Joseph*, points out the early midrashic interpretation of
Gen. 37.2 ('These are the generations of JACOB; JOSEPH was seventeen years old when he was shepherding the flock with his
brothers') where the unusual juxtaposition of names is taken to
mean that Joseph is like his father in all things (1997: 250). Of
course, Jacob is the other patriarchal figure whose story hinges on
the theme of exile forced by conflict among brothers. Neither
Joseph nor Jacob is seen as blameless. *Genesis Rabbah* 84.7 comments (on the same verse [Gen. 37.2]): 'He was seventeen years
old, yet [the text] says he was a "youth"? But this means he did
deeds of youthful foolishness: he bedaubed his eyes and smoothed
back his hair and raised his heel,' to which Kugel comments,
'Joseph's immature behavior while shepherding with his brothers,
alluded to in Scripture's use of the single word "youth", thus provided yet another good reason for his brothers' hatred' (p. 251).
*Tanḥuma* makes the connection between Joseph's narcissistic behavior in his father's house and its replication in Egypt and in fact
sees it as causal for Joseph's fall from Potiphar's grace:

> When Joseph found himself so comfortably situated, he began to
> eat and drink well, to frizz his hair, and to say, 'Blessed be He who
> is everywhere, who helped me forget my father's house.' Then the
> Holy One said to Joseph: Your father is mourning for you in sack-
> cloth and ashes, and you eat and drink well, and frizz your hair—
> you pampered brat! As you live, I shall sic a she-bear on you. At once,
> 'it came to pass that his master's wife cast her eyes upon Joseph'
> (Gen. 39.7) (Bialik and Ravnitsky 1992: 52).

Frederick Buechner's recent novel, *The Son of Laughter* (1993), a
sensitive retelling of the Jacob saga, builds a convincing scenario
in which Joseph de facto comes almost to play the part of a son in
the childless Potiphar household, and where the disastrous event

that brings the naive idyll to an end is tinged as much with symbolic incest as with the threat of adultery.[5]

## Destitution Stage

Pérez Firmat's second stage of exile, that of destitution, is one in which 'the awareness of displacement crushes the fantasy of rootedness' (1994: 10). Among the many factors that can bring about such an awareness of being displaced, none is perhaps more frequent or disturbing in the experience of exiles than the experience of being 'put in one's place' by the prejudices and stereotypes of the dominant culture, which often entails as well falling foul of its legal establishment.

Genesis 39.6 describes young Joseph as 'fair of form and fair to look at' (Fox 1995: 187) in the verse that serves as a prologue to the incident with Potiphar's wife. Midrashic elaboration makes him so handsome that Potiphar's wife takes to changing her clothes three times a day so that he will notice. In one memorable incident she calls him into the room where she along with some other Egyptian matrons are peeling citrons, whereupon her friends, dumbstruck at Joseph's beauty, all cut their hands (Bialik and Ravnitsky 1992: 52, citing *Tanḥuma*). Potiphar's wife, no doubt herself a stereotypical figure in the narrative, nevertheless easily resorts to stereotyping Joseph, first as a sexual object. Seen from and by the new center, the exile is cast in a stereotypic role which he or she did not choose, not so much a simple sexual temptation, as rabbinic exegesis has traditionally read the incident, but an attack on his or her dignity and autonomy that we today would rather define as sexual harassment. Did the Egyptians have equivalents of the 'Latin lover' or of the 'hot-blooded *señorita*' stereotypes for Hebrews? Do those of us who have come to view history—and to read the Bible—with 'noninnocent' eyes,[6] who know the suffocating terror of people in the periphery forced to play roles they did not seek or create by the power that the center assumes over them understand Joseph's predicament in a specially gripping way?

Potiphar's wife's discourse has a flip side, moreover, that she exhibits when Joseph rejects her advances. It is significant that

---

5.  See especially chs. 21, 'The Naked Boy', and 22, 'The White Kilt'.
6.  The term is derived from Justo González (1990); see especially ch. 5, 'Reading the Bible in Spanish'.

Joseph then becomes 'a Hebrew man' and 'the Hebrew servant' in the self-justifying words she utters in Gen. 39.14 and 17 and that she begins to refer to herself as 'us', in other words to identify Joseph as the Hebrew 'other' against her stance within the Egyptian 'us'. Later in the story, Pharaoh's baker, who has forgotten Joseph after returning to the court from the jail where Joseph served him daily and correctly interpreted his dream, likewise refers to him as 'a Hebrew lad there with us' (Gen. 40.12). The exile is 'the other': the outsider, the alien, when seen from and by the center, and exiles know how easily, as a class of aliens, they can be demonized or relegated to oblivion, or, in other words, submerged into an imposed group identity.

*Institution Stage*
On the other hand, people who live in diaspora enjoy the problematic advantage of being bicultural, at the same time belonging and not belonging to two different worlds. Just as I have become a Cuban-American, so Joseph became a Hebrew-Egyptian, so thoroughly at home, at least in the externals of Egyptian culture, that by the denouement of the story his constructed identity functions as a successful disguise to fool his own brothers. The narrative in fact turns Joseph into an Egyptian before the reader's eyes by specifying a number of details which, in the aggregate, construct his new identity.

As he comes near Pharaoh, who clearly represents the center of power in Egyptian society, Joseph will shave and dress like an Egyptian (Gen. 41.14), and, as Pharaoh recognizes and rewards his talent, he will come to bear an Egyptian name, to speak fluently in Egyptian, to eat like an Egyptian. In short, Joseph becomes almost indistinguishable from an Egyptian. He is decorated by Pharaoh and given a position of supreme power in the land. He even marries an Egyptian woman, Asenath, the daughter of Poti Fera, priest of On, and begets sons whom he names 'Menashe/He-Who-Makes-Forget, meaning: God has made-me-forget all my hardships, all my father's house' and 'Efrayim/Double Fruit, meaning: God has made me bear fruit in the land of my affliction', as Everett Fox translates Gen. 41.51, 52 (1995: 198). As many critics have put it, the price for Joseph's survival—not to say success—in Egypt is assimilation. Aaron Wildavsky, who compares Joseph unfavorably on this point with such figures as Esther and Daniel (he calls the latter 'a satire on Joseph'), says that in Genesis 41,

> Pharaoh, in sum, marries Joseph to Egypt. Pharaoh puts his signet ring on Joseph's hand as a husband would on a bride. He dresses him in finery and gives him jewelry, the gold necklace of office, as befits a bride. He gives him a new name as a wife takes on the name of her husband. By marrying Joseph to the family of his god, Pharaoh seeks supremacy over both the man and his God. Pharaoh marries, clothes, adorns, and names Joseph, everything, it seems, but literally giving birth to him as a new Egyptian man (Wildavsky 1993: 125).

What this analysis misses is the 'hyphenation' of Joseph, his ability to become not 'a new Egyptian man' but a 'Hebrew-Egyptian', not assimilated but biculturated. Pérez Firmat reaches a very different verdict when he analyzes Ricky Ricardo, Desi Arnaz's Cuban-American persona in the 'I Love Lucy' television series, whom he calls

> the tutelary spirit, the *orisha* of Cuban-American culture. He embodies an openness to otherness, a liking for unlikeness that defines Cuban America as a whole. By loving Lucy, Desi renounces regression, using the word in both the sense of *regreso* and *regresión*. As Ricky himself stated, to love Lucy is to embrace the unfamiliar in the form of an americana who stands, more generally, for Americana (1994: 12).

On the other hand, he says later,

> There is no denying that by loving Lucy Ricky distances himself from his native language and culture; in this respect he becomes 'less' Cuban. Perhaps biculturation always entails some degree of deculturation. What Ricky gets in return, though, is a renewed self compacted from his Cuban past and his Cuban-American present. New and old selves relate as childhood and adulthood, or infancy and maturity. Being half Cuban, Ricky becomes a whole man. This Cuban-American self is certainly not an easy or stable achievement, and it requires constant struggle against encroachments from both sides. Regression remains a constant temptation, as does assimilation. It is not always easy for Ricky to give Ricardo his due, and vice versa (1994: 44).

Both of these judgments about Ricky, the Cuban-American character apply, *mutatis mutandis*, to the character of Joseph the Hebrew-Egyptian. At 17, Joseph was a Hebrew slave, a marginal foreigner sold by his brothers into slavery in Egypt. At 30, he has constructed a new identity: he is a powerful Hebrew-Egyptian, a hyphenated self doing the—to me—long familiar balancing act between regression and acculturation. Familiar, particularly, because it was for him—as for Ricky, for Gustavo Pérez, or for me—also familial. Claus Westermann summarizes the judgment of many traditional historical critics about the Joseph narrative, who, following H. Gressmann, read the story as 'a family story into which a 'political narrative'...is inserted' (1986: 24). For a Cuban-American reader of the Joseph story, such a judgment is neither necessary nor warranted, because, as Roberto Goizueta has put it,

> for Latinos and Latinas, the understanding of human action, or praxis, must include our active participation in all of our relationships, both private and public, both interpersonal and institutional, both natural and supernatural. Praxis is life as lived, i.e., 'lived experience'. Thus, praxis involves not only social and political action but also our common, 'private', day-to-day struggle for survival in an alien environment (1995: 112).

That, however, just scratches the surface of a much more complex cultural and intellectual phenomenon that all exiles, as hyphenated people, more or less consciously undergo. One aspect of that phenomenon is that, from the margin, one can see things that the center cannot see about itself, and this can work out to the benefit of both center and margin. While Joseph piously ascribes to God the ability to interpret dreams, it is clear that he is the one furnishing those interpretations, whatever the ultimate source. Why were the skilled dream interpreters of Egypt not able to interpret Pharaoh's dream, while Joseph was? The double dream is after all rather clear in its meaning. Perhaps because Joseph the slave did not have the investment in preserving his status at the court that probably prevented the Pharaoh's 'establishment' dream interpreters from telling him the obvious truth, a truth that seemed to threaten the Pharaoh's status as guarantor of the fertility of Egypt. Once again, midrashic interpretation (*Gen. R.* 89.6) adumbrated the agenda that crippled the Egyptian sages' interpretation of Pharaoh's dream:

> 'But there was none that could interpret them unto Pharaoh' (Gen. 41.8). R. Joshua of Sikhnin said in the name of R. Levi: They

did interpret them, but Pharaoh did not like what they said. For example, they said: The seven fat cows mean that you will beget seven daughters; the seven lean cows mean that you will bury seven daughters. Or: The seven full ears of corn mean that you will conquer seven principalities; the seven thin ears that seven principalities will rebel against you.

What was the purpose of all of this? So that Joseph would come at the end and be raised to high rank. For the Holy One said: If Joseph were to come right away and interpret the dream, he would not receive the recognition that should be his. The magicians would say to Pharaoh, 'Had you asked us, we would at once have interpreted the dream for you in the same sense'. Therefore He waited for the magicians to wear themselves out in their attempts and to exhaust Pharaoh's spirit, until Joseph would come and restore it (Bialik and Ravnitsky 1992: 52-53).

The obsequious willingness of the Egyptian magicians to tell the Pharaoh what they thought he wanted to hear made them incapable of either seeing or telling the truth. Joseph the Hebrew, however, who had grown up in the 'Third World' of his time rather than in prosperous Egypt, understood better than they the urgency of the warning of the coming famine that the dream proclaimed. When Joseph, therefore, says to his brothers that 'it was to save life that God sent me on before you' (Gen. 45.5), he is speaking of the life of Egypt, as well as that of his own people. In Genesis 41 Pharaoh is the first to recognize the gift of insight and perspective about their common problems that the margin can offer the center: he is the first to listen to Joseph, not now as a foreign dream interpreter but as a wise advisor. Justo González has said that there may be a dislocation of interpretive point of view, if we only assume that, given that Joseph is the hero of the story, we are all simply to identify with him:

It is possible that those doing the interpretation...should read the story placing themselves, not in the sandals of Joseph, but rather in the shoes of the Pharaoh. In that case, the text no longer speaks so much about how good Christians ought to try to influence the powerful, but rather about how the powerful—particularly if they seek to do the will of God—must seek the alien, discover their gifts, and seek whatever wisdom and guidance those gifts might offer (1996: 96).

## Concluding Comments

To read Joseph's story is to read a story of exile and alienation, of loss and deception, of oppression and of pain. It is the story of many diasporas, over many centuries and across many borders, whose members, like the exiles who wrote it and first treasured it, have loved it for its realistic portrayal of the dangers of their situation, but ultimately for its affirmation of the hope that their pilgrimage will somehow turn out for the best, that 'it was to save life'. And for them—for me—the story is also a story of survival and success, of reunion and reconciliation, in a word, of salvation. Stories such as this remind us also that 'José' is a human being and not a stereotype, who, given a chance, may contribute considerably more than we can imagine to our common good.

BIBLIOGRAPHY

Behar, Ruth
    1996            *The Vulnerable Observer: Anthropology that Breaks your Heart* (Boston: Beacon Press).
Bialik, Hayim Nahman, and Yehoshua Hana Ravnitsky
    1992            *The Book of Legends: Sefer Ha-Aggadah: Legends from the Talmud and the Midrash* (New York: Schocken Books).
Boyarin, Daniel
    1994            *A Radical Jew: Paul and the Politics of Identity* (Berkeley: University of California Press).
Boyarin, Daniel, and Jonathan Boyarin
    1993            'Diaspora: Generation and the Ground of Jewish Identity', *Critical Inquiry* 19: 693-725.
Buechner, Frederick
    1993            *The Son of Laughter* (San Francisco: HarperCollins).
Coats, George W.
    1983            *Genesis: With an Introduction to Narrative Literature* (Grand Rapids: Eerdmans).
Fox, Everett
    1995            *The Five Books of Moses* (New York: Schocken Books).
García-Treto, Francisco
    1996            'Joseph in Exile: A Personal Testimony', in Public Affairs Television, *Talking About Genesis: A Resource Guide* (New York: Doubleday Main Street Books): 145-48.
Goizueta, Roberto S.
    1995            *Caminemos con Jesús: Toward a Hispanic/Latino Theology of Accompaniment* (Maryknoll, NY: Orbis Books).

González, Justo L.
1990        *Mañana: Christian Theology from a Hispanic Perspective* (Nashville: Abingdon Press).
1996        *Santa Biblia: The Bible through Hispanic Eyes* (Nashville: Abingdon Press).
Kugel, James L.
1997        *The Bible as It Was* (Cambridge, MA: Belknap Press of Harvard University).
Pérez Firmat, Gustavo
1994        *Life on the Hyphen: The Cuban-American Way* (Austin: University of Texas Press).
1995        *Next Year in Cuba: A Cubano's Coming-of-Age in America* (New York: Anchor Books Doubleday).
Rieff, David
1993        *The Exile: Cuba in the Heart of Miami* (New York: Simon & Schuster).
Segovia, Fernando F.
1995        'Toward a Hermeneutics of the Diaspora: A Hermeneutics of Otherness and Engagement', in Fernando F. Segovia and Mary Ann Tolbert (eds.), *Reading from This Place*. I. *Social Location and Biblical Interpretation* (Minneapolis: Fortress Press): 57-73.
Westermann, Claus
1986        *Genesis 37–50: A Commentary* (Minneapolis: Augsburg).
Wildavsky, Aaron
1993        *Assimilation Versus Separation: Joseph the Administrator and the Politics of Religion in Biblical Israel* (New Brunswick: Transaction Publishers).
Zornberg, Avivah Gottlieb
1995        *Genesis: The Beginning of Desire* (Philadelphia: Jewish Publication Society).

# Subversive Promises and the Creation of a Parallel Sphere: Divine Encounters with Hagar and Rebekah

HEMCHAND GOSSAI

## Introduction

I undertake the following discussion from the perspective of one who has been shaped by different religious and cultural environments. My great-grandparents came from India to work as indentured servants in the British colony of British Guiana. My formative years were spent in a Hindu environment in British Guiana and then in the independent state of Guyana; my later years as a Christian were spent living and studying in the United States and Europe. My interest in issues of marginality within the biblical material is directly connected to these experiences.

Is there a place for an exile within a land of the chosen? Will an exile always remain an exile and always be identified as an exile? Is there a future for one who dwells in the shadows? Can divine promises be given to those who do not only function away from the center but are in fact in conflict with the center?

There is a clear sense that the God of primeval history in the opening chapters of Genesis is also the God who seeks and promises a future to the exile or slave, to the one who challenges societal conventions. Those on the margin are not ultimately allowed to languish on the outside without a future, without a promise. Even one like Hagar, who is doubly victimized, is granted a promise, a spoken word that announces a radical future hitherto unimagined. Rebekah, concerned about her pregnancy, takes up the matter directly with God, and the particularity of her internal struggle—which only she, and not Isaac, can fully appreciate—is heard by God and placed within a larger universal context.

Rebekah understands. The promises that are thus given to Hagar and Rebekah are for generations and shape the future as a result. In neither encounter is there a moral judgment as to which of the two futures will be better. There is a clear indication that the covenant established with the one in the center does not in any way exhaust the possibilities of additional relationships beyond the center. When we hear of the divine message given to Rebekah, immediately we as readers are led to think in a certain direction. To be sure, the message is given to Rebekah and concerns Jacob and Esau, but there is also a much grander interest at work here: this is not only a familial story but also a story of two nations, two peoples.

In this essay I propose that, as divine promises are pronounced in these ancestral narratives of Genesis, there is a distinct and intentional establishment of provisions for concurrent and seemingly conflictual stories. At one level, it would appear that God is subverting the very thing that God sets out to establish. As if the journeys of Abraham and Sarah, Isaac and Rebekah, were not challenging enough in and of themselves, parallel journeys of conflict are also created and must be reckoned with. That is, the promises made to Abraham and Sarah and carried on through their descendants are assumed to be and are in fact established as the central promises. There is, however, nothing in the text that preempts other promises being made that would parallel the ones at the center. What is striking about the parallel sets of promises is that inherently the bearers and descendants of the promises are in conflict. This conflict is established at the outset by God, and there is no textual indication that the conflicts are designed to determine winners and losers; rather, the indication is that people who live together with varying degrees of power often function in conflict.

It is not so much that the text indicates the moral value of conflict or the relative goodness of the promises. In fact, there is much evidence to suggest that the central promise-bearers are flawed characters. The characters—Abraham, Sarah, Isaac, Jacob, Hagar or Ishmael—are not in themselves evil or good, and the promises that they bear are not predicated on their personal characteristics. The Genesis narratives provide for us a tapestry of human and divine relations that are woven and interwoven in complex, delicate and sometimes inseparable ways. These narratives do not allow us to rest easily—they are far from being linear, straightforward, unidimensional. Even though the focus of this essay will be on Hagar and Rebekah, Ishmael and Jacob, we must also reckon with Esau and Isaac, Abraham and Sarah, and the other players within the story. At least, within this discussion, there are no villains and evil characters. We cannot overlook the agony of Sarah and Abraham; we cannot overlook the pain of Isaac and Esau. Human stories are complex. For societal conventions such as the role of primogeniture to be challenged, it is not necessary to cast Esau as the firstborn in an evil or, for that matter, even unfavorable light.

## Complexity of Human Stories

Let me illustrate what I am talking about. What do we do with Esau? For the direction that I am proposing, it is not necessary to destroy Esau and characterize him as evil or bad or any such. I would suggest otherwise. Gerald Janzen argues,

> It is that Esau is a non reflective sort, given to action—one who likes to hunt, eat and move on, as in the present instance: 'he ate, he drank, he rose, he went his way, he despised his birthright'. He lacks the patience for delayed satisfactions that is to be a quality or spiritual characteristic of the new people that Yahweh is in the process of fashioning (1993: 96).

However, there is little that one could find to support the notion that delayed satisfaction is a moral quality necessary for spiritual leadership. As we are able to see throughout the biblical tradition, many who would be leaders and promise-bearers are anything but patient.

Burton Visotzky concludes, 'Esau does not exactly savor his meal. Rather Genesis reports with four brief Hebrew words, "he ate, drank, rose, left"' (1996: 138). Even though these verbs might remind one of 'veni, vidi, vinci' in terms of their unreflective character, they cannot be dismissed simply on the basis of the convention or the possibility that they do not fit the hermeneutical direction we have chosen. Whatever one might say about the savoring of a meal and all of the sensual overtones of a meal eaten deliberately—and there is certainly a place for that—the fact is that 'three-martini lunches' are not for the starving and hungry.

The very text and the staccato expression underline the fundamental difference between the basic situation of hunger and the sensual joy of lingering over a meal. For Esau, the urgency and immediacy of hunger, and its extended consequences, have taken precedence over the role of the birthright and its future possibilities. Hunger as an expression of weakness and poverty is the occasion for the exchange of the birthright. As a systemic issue, hunger is expressly in the domain of the poor and marginalized. The relative importance of wealth, power or birthright is relegated to a secondary status in the face of hunger or famine.

These Genesis narratives are received by the reader in a variety of ways. They cannot be read and received in a vacuum. The reader—particularly readers whose experience marks them as slaves, exiles, refugees, disenfranchised or marginalized persons—bring to the text a different and, I would submit, perfectly legitimate perspective. For example, commenting on the use of Hagar by Sarah and the deafening silence of Hagar, Bharati Mukherjee voices with existential integrity what many experience and thus must bring to the reading of these narratives: 'Those of us who have experienced class prejudice and colonialism can be forgiven for reading into this omission the sad, silenced issues of disenfranchisement' (1996: 101).

Historically, scholarly research and attention have concentrated on the characters who constitute the main plot and on the central themes in these narratives. Thus, the principal focus has been on the patriarchs—Abraham, Isaac and Jacob. Feminist scholarship, particularly in the last two decades, has forged new and significant directions in terms of the multilayered fabric of the narratives and the essential role of women. Among others, Hagar and Rebekah have been given much-needed attention. Yet even here there has been a reluctance or, perhaps more accurately, an inability to give to their persons and their roles the radically new directions that are essential. Somehow, the notion has held fast that one cannot speak well of Hagar or Rebekah without soiling the conventions. Just as there has been timidity in assigning blame to Sarah and seeing her as responsible, along with Abraham, for the plight of Hagar, so has Rebekah been consistently viewed as one who shows favoritism and is deceitful.

Yet one might read these texts with great integrity and see clearly that Rebekah was doing precisely what was expected of her, given what was entrusted to her from God. As was the social custom, and believing Esau to be the firstborn and thus the recipient of the family's birthright, the aged Isaac seeks to pass on the all-important blessing from father to son. Equally importantly, Rebekah, as the sole recipient of another promise that is given in secrecy and that will challenge and undermine social convention, must ensure that she does what is necessary, using whatever means at her disposal. In many respects, her 'chosenness' brings with it a great deal of agony. Ultimately, at the risk of sounding utilitarian, I would suggest that she makes excruciating sacrifices for the sake of what is known only to her, as well as for the sake of the greater good.

In doing what she must do, Rebekah acts contrary to her maternal instinct. It is not a matter of favoritism. Challenging the status quo and societal convention and disrupting the comfort zone for the sake of divine promise-keeping is not favoritism. Indeed, one of the factors frequently neglected in most discussions about Rebekah is her self-sacrifice. At the very core of her being, through divine initiative, she is made to choose between her sons, and she is given no choice. She sacrifices what is at the very core of a mother's being, that is, her instinctive, even fiercely protective love of her children. Rebekah stands to gain nothing from doing what she does. In many respects, she is the embodiment of sacrifice. Those readers who see Rebekah as having ulterior motives, I submit, miss the radicality of what is at work. Naomi Steinberg suggests, 'Rebekah already knows that Jacob will dominate his brother Esau. Thus she intends to secure the loyalty of Jacob in order that he will use his future power to her benefit' (1993: 91). This sort of view is textually untenable, since in no way is Rebekah a beneficiary. What the promise to Rebekah entails and what Rebekah does is simply to call into question the manner in which power within society is distributed and executed. Rebekah's actions in halting the convention did not so much establish a new custom but rather gave shape to a new dimension of the status quo. The promise of the ancestors will continue, but not as expected or designed. Those who would fall back on the notion that 'this is the way it has always been' will now have to reckon with new realities.

Much has been written on these narratives, and within this important framework additional hermeneutical strands have emerged. These narratives continue to provide for us a rich and virtually inexhaustible source of meaning for contemporary circumstances. I would submit that these narratives have redemptive value for contemporary society, although they do not make for easy interpretation, given all of the social prisms through which we view them. Yet responsibility dictates that we must seek. There is a triumph of grace in these stories, for the outsiders are allowed to shape their futures to some degree. Despite the roles of Abraham and Sarah and the status of the firstborn, God protects and grants a future.

Both Hagar and Rebekah are the recipients of what might be termed divine secrets, and, while there is some evidence that Hagar and God spoke with Abraham regarding Ishmael, in the case of Rebekah she is the sole bearer of the pronouncement, 'Two nations are in your womb, and two peoples born of you shall be divided, the one shall be stronger than the other, the elder shall serve the younger' (Gen. 25.23). In both instances, promises are given that appear to undermine the ongoing central promise. These two women did not seek out God with these promises in mind, nor for that matter did they have any other specific promise in mind. They are taken unawares by what God says, and the promises are accepted without argument or discussion. Both know that what has transpired will not be fulfilled routinely. There will be hardships: Hagar will return to the very household where she was brutalized; Rebekah will take whatever curse comes with Jacob and will embrace whatever sacrifice. Neither Hagar nor Rebekah speaks much; indeed, in the case of Hagar, as reflective of her status, she is not allowed a voice. Yet when both she and Rebekah speak, what they have to say is enough to confirm the fact that they are both God's chosen also. Both will face daunting challenges, and both will proceed with courage.

One also must note that while both Hagar and Rebekah function away from the center, their experiences are clearly not uniformly the same. The experiences of exiles, slaves, marginalized persons cannot be engaged as if they were all uniformly the same.

Each person brings his or her experiences and circumstances to bear and give shape to his or her own narrative within the framework of the marginalized. Hagar and Rebekah are given two very different promises, and what eventuates with Ishmael and Jacob reflects this difference. Pitzele declares, 'For a time Sarah is upstaged by her auxiliary; the pregnant Hagar displaces her mistress' (1995: 108). Yet there is no real displacement here. Hagar never did take the place or could ever take the place of Sarah. Her importance is not to be understood in displacement. While it was Sarah's idea to use Hagar as a surrogate, there is no textual evidence to suggest or support the notion that the surrogate displaces the mistress.

## Power, Identity and Conflict

The narrative in Genesis 16 begins with the naming of three characters—Sarai, Abram and Hagar. With immediacy in the first two verses, the problem is named, responsibility for Sarah's barrenness is ascribed to Yahweh, and the solution is sought in the person of Hagar, the fertile Egyptian slave woman. Within the continuum of powerlessness, Sarah represents the center of oppressed people, while it might be said that Hagar represents those who are on the periphery. One of the very troubling features of this type of gradation is that the oppressed at a more central level begin to treat the oppressed at a more marginalized level with the same disdain and contempt that they received.

   In the eyes of Sarah, Hagar simply provides for her something missing in her own life over which she has no control. In the estimation of Sarah, the One who *does* have control has chosen not to exercise that control by granting her the fulfillment she seeks in the timeline *she* has decided on. There is no inkling in Sarah's plan that Hagar's identity will be any different from what it is at present, and certainly no hint that there will be a fundamental transformation in Hagar after conception. The idea that Sarah's God, who is yet to fulfill his promise to Sarah and Abraham, would make promises to this slave woman is not at all entertained. Clearly, Sarah's unidimensional plan leaves no room for the possibility of a new future with a transformed Hagar. There is little doubt that it never crossed Sarah's mind that Yahweh, her God as well as that of Abraham, would seek out Hagar and bestow on her a future apart from Sarah and Abraham.

It is assumed that Hagar, as a slave, is entirely at the disposal of her mistress. Sarah was demonstrating that she was capable of achieving that which Yahweh had naturally prevented her from doing (v. 2a). Like Sarah, Hagar surely understands the importance of an heir. However, given her status as slave, with no framework for an opportunity to have offspring, she holds tightly to the chance that she has at her disposal. Even though the act against Hagar treats her as a nonentity, the occasion opens for her a dream that she dared not have dreamt before: the unthinkable becomes thinkable and the impossible appears possible. Hagar does not have the power to challenge the convention, though unwittingly, through Sarah's actions, she will do precisely that. While Sarah considers the occasion a way of building herself up, she fails to consider that the slave woman might also have such daring hopes for herself. That Hagar would want to build herself up is simply never entertained. This view says as much about the representatives at the center as about the limitations placed upon God.

While Sarah is fearful of the newly transformed Hagar, she is not willing to recognize fully her own initiative in the matter. The issue is no longer the longing for a child, but rather the challenge to the status quo and to those who constitute the status quo. Some recognize the power in Hagar that is absent in Sarah and, at this point in her life, beyond her reach. Sarah's interest in an offspring now assumes a secondary role, as conveyed by her willingness and interest in banishing Hagar and the unborn child. The challenge of power becomes the crux at this point in the narrative.

Abraham assures Sarah that she has the power to do that which is *good in her eyes*. This is essentially a *carte blanche* statement to use one's power. With Hagar in a powerless state and cast into the role of instigator, she is left without recourse. Abraham must be saddled with responsibility here, since he is aware of Sarah's fear and anger but still suggests that she determine the nature of the punishment on the basis of what she considers good! Essentially, Abraham washes his hands of the matter and allows Sarah to be the one to have 'hands stained with blood'. Sarah, like Lady Macbeth, began this scenario with a plan in mind, and, as the plot disintegrates, it is she who has bloodstained hands. On the other hand, Abraham like Pilate attempts to 'wash his hands' of the matter, although, by not acting with his inherent power, he becomes deeply embroiled in the episode himself and must be held accountable as well. Even before witnessing the result of Sarah's actions, one is placed on alert by Sarah's previous action in inviting Abraham to lie with Hagar. We are aware that she might be incapable of dealing wisely and fairly with Hagar. Whatever else one might think of Sarah in this context, she is not in a position to make a good judgment. As a slave, it is clear that Hagar was not Sarah's equal, and the first remote sign of equal status between the two created an overtly adversarial atmosphere.

While the immediate issue at stake in the Hagar narrative is centered on the quest for a son, and the degree to which Sarah pursued this, a larger matter calls us to recognize the fact that the 'outsider' is used to fulfill the needs and desires of the 'insider'. The use of Hagar goes beyond surrogacy, beyond ethnicity and tradition. So strong is Sarah's urge for a child that she is willing to overlook any such issue regarding Hagar. Moreover, to be a slave is to be fully owned. There is, in reality, no component in a slave's life that belongs exclusively to the slave. The entire being of the slave is at the disposal of the owner. More than anything, Hagar as an 'outsider' needed hospitality from the community in general, and from Sarah and Abraham in particular. As if being a slave were not demeaning enough, Hagar becomes the object of additional hostility at the hands of her mistress.

The indifference to Hagar as a person in her own right is evident throughout the narrative. Even though Sarah is the one who initiates the plan, she never refers to Hagar by name. Indeed, Sarah only refers to Hagar and Ishmael by their social status, not by name. Hagar is never considered as another woman. It is the narrator who names Hagar. Thus, right from the start, Hagar's identity is made incomplete through the absence of her name on the lips of Sarah. The name is at the heart and soul of the person. Naming identifies a person and allows us to know and experience him or her. The naming of Ishmael might very well embody the greater promise. The particularity of Ishmael's name bears a universal promise to all who cry to God. In the midst of the circumstances of life, *God hears* (Ishmael) is a real promise. Yet this is a hope that must exist in the realm of conventional human power structures. The promise consists not in eliminating the sources of power (imperial, economic, political, and so forth) but in functioning confidently within such structures. There is nothing facile about the promise. It will, in fact, necessitate courage. In this way, there continues to be a tension between suffering and hope.

The stark and telling difference between human and divine recognition of one's personhood is seen in 16.8, where Hagar is addressed by name by the angel of Yahweh. Even as a slave, an outsider, an oppressed person, a wilderness refugee, Hagar has an identity that is divinely given. She is not allowed to cry out against the double injustice of concubinage and slavery done to her; she is muted by the two sources of power between whom she is caught. The reality is that she is without voice, unable to speak a language of power and domination, and without human advocacy. The oppressed is left voiceless. The only voice in these opening verses is that of Sarah, and she orders Abraham to act. Abraham, who is clearly in a position to decide justly what is right and wrong, listens to the voice of power and proceeds from that point. Clearly, the issue of Hagar's silence has far-reaching implications. Yahweh does what Abraham and Sarah fail to do, namely, to enter into conversation with Hagar. Westermann suggests,

> by the greeting and inquiry, the messenger takes part in Hagar's lot; he accepts her into the realm of *Shalom*. He enables her to make a trustful response and show herself ready to accept the word of this stranger. That this unknown one speaks her name indicates that he is an 'other', one who knows; his friendly attention to Hagar evokes her trustful reply (1985: 244).

The questioning by the messenger of Yahweh reveals that Hagar does have an identity but that it is tied to Sarah. It is true, as Trible remarks, that the questions by the messenger 'embody origin and destiny' (1984: 15). Yet Hagar's answer suggests that there is no place of origin but a slaveowner from whom she is fleeing and no certainty of destination as her presence in the wilderness testifies. Hagar the slave woman has become a refugee, fleeing injustice and finding herself in a purgatorial world. The messenger recognizes that Hagar's destiny is tied to Sarah—as painful as it may be, that is the reality. Thus, the issue at stake is one of restoration and reconciliation in the midst of inequities, injustice and power struggles.

When Yahweh orders Hagar to return and submit to Sarah, one might be led to conclude that Yahweh is acting on the side of the powerful and seeking to uphold the status quo. At one level, it does not appear to make much sense, particularly given the overall direction of the biblical material, which places God unquestionably on the side of the poor. The irony is that the poor and the powerless, arguably more than any other group, need a voice, and yet they are the ones who are made voiceless. While Hagar is not allowed to participate in the decision-making by the angel of Yahweh, the decision and promise regarding her future, she is in fact in dialogue with the angel. One cannot read of Hagar's situation and not think of those who live among us who are oppressed and voiceless. Who will provoke on their behalf? Both Hagar and Rebekah are given promises about offsprings who will provoke the system and the dwellers at the center and will indeed, in the contemporary sense of the word, become provokers.

It is not difficult to draw parallels between the sending back of Hagar to Sarah and the plight of modern-day refugees. Common to our existence is the presence of political and economic refugees, huddled together in boats and warehouses, held in barracks and foreign lands, only to be told, after having spent time in this 'in-between' world, that they must return to their place of origin. There appears to be no justice when humans are forced by other humans, shaped by power structures, to remain in bondage.

So what does the encounter between Hagar and Yahweh establish? The future of Hagar, which includes a son and many descendants, will be forged out of a life of submission and slavery. In the face of hostility, Hagar will not only survive but live, and be destined for a future, albeit through her son. The description of Ishmael's nature demonstrates that he will in fact not live, like his mother, as a slave. As Ishmael grew in the household of Sarah and Abraham, he must have been aware of the oppression that he and his mother faced. One cannot help but conclude that this kind of oppression and affliction are intrinsic in shaping children as they grow into adulthood. As is so often the case, the one who is the recipient of oppression learns that this is the way to live and survive. The conflict that will come to characterize the life of Ishmael can be explained through his experience in the household of Sarah and Abraham. The return of Hagar to Sarah is not a return to the status quo. While the messenger's words might appear to be a reconstruction of an identical slave–mistress relationship as existed before, in fact Hagar is now aligned with a different source of power. Hagar now has the confidence of Yahweh, and, while Sarah and Abraham are covenanted with Yahweh, Yahweh's 'preferential option' for the poor is evident here.

While Rebekah is never told not to discuss Yahweh's words to her, that is essentially what happens, and so de facto she too is voiceless, though, because of circumstances, self-imposed. Part of the critical role of voicelessness on the part of the outsider is the reality that societal norm dictates that such be the case. It is not that Rebekah is afraid or weak. Indeed, there is evidence right from the start that in many respects Rebekah is more forthright than Isaac, and certainly more adept at cleverly executing her plans. It is Rebekah who is concerned about her pregnancy, yet she does not speak with Isaac about it but rather goes directly to Yahweh. Janzen observes,

> Rebekah inquires of Yahweh who announces a destiny that has its roots already in her womb. Is this destiny foreordained by God? Do the twins struggle already in the womb because God has set them and their futures against each other? (1993: 95)

Rebekah also must confront and deal with her internal conflict. One could surmise that there is a tearing apart of her maternal feelings for both sons and her loyalty to the promise versus her sense of loyalty to share what she knows with Isaac. Rebekah has the power of knowledge, for she knows that God has selected Jacob and that she is the one chosen to bear that knowledge, and this by itself has the potential for conflict. Not all knowledge brings freedom. Some knowledge brings pain and anxiety. Since her knowledge will lead to the challenging of the conventions, Rebekah will have to find a means of carrying out the task. To some, Rebekah's actions might seem as nothing short of treachery and disloyalty, yet of course there is no chastisement or condemnation or curse by God. Rebekah is God's deputy, and she does what in her view is the thing to do.

Ishmael and Jacob, while offsprings of the parallel promises and principal architects in challenging the conventions, including the role of primogeniture, will proceed in very different directions. Ishmael is described as one who will be fearless and combative, not only against the enemy but also against his own kin. Jacob is not described thus. Whether in his encounter with Laban or with Esau, he resorts to trickery and deceit rather than force. This is not to say that he is reticent, for one need only recall the encounter in the night when he refuses to allow the being to depart without bestowing on him a blessing. Rosenberg and Bloom describe it as follows,

> Jacob is fleeing from the consequences of his (and Rebecca's) hoax, and in that flight he does receive the first fruit of his usurpation. Yahweh stands next to him and speaks to him as familiarly as he spoke to Abram (1990: 214).

Jacob's all-night encounter with the nameless divine being is symbolic at different levels. It would be easy to say somewhat reductionistically that this was a harmless struggle. The one who has usurped and undermined the convention will be confirmed with a name change, but it will happen in the dark of the night where the divine being appears and disappears anonymously. Even though not in the same way, Ishmael is also named by God, indeed the only person in Genesis who is named by God, and this naming is also revealed away from the routine of everyday life. It is given in the wilderness. It is clear that the futures of Ishmael and Jacob, received through the promises, will be marked by conflict, one in the wilderness and the other confirmed in the dark of night while wrestling. Indeed, for the promise to proceed, conflict will become the prime feature to be employed and then resolved. Brueggemann captures the reality of the conflict with Jacob succinctly and clearly when he concludes,

> The conflict with Jacob is a conflict not with 'spiritual' realities, but with the ways in which human life has been institutionalized. Primogeniture is not simply one rule among many. It is the linchpin of an entire social and legal system which defines rights and privileges and provides a way around internecine disputes. But that same practice which protects the order of society is also a way of destining some to advantage and others to disadvantage (1982: 209).

The conflict that will characterize the life and legacy of Ishmael is not spelled out, but it is mentioned in a somewhat casual and general way. It is as if to suggest that this is simply the way it is for the one who will have to function from the outside. We are told that Ishmael will be 'a wild ass of a man', and Jacob, as we discover, will be at great odds with his brother and his uncle Laban. These are two scenarios of conflict singled out for Jacob, and so, like Ishmael, he too will function from the vantage point of conflict. One is left to wonder whether in both of these cases we have an accurate prediction by God that Ishmael and Jacob will prevail through their own resources and strength, despite such conflict. Even though conflict will be the primary mode of being in the case of both Ishmael and Jacob, both of their mothers, to whom the specific promises are given, dialogue with the divine. Those who function on the margin are not simply relegated to the state of the voiceless by the divine.

The election of Jacob overturns the role of primogeniture and, in so doing, discards the notion, both ancient and contemporary, that good is rewarded and evil is punished. Not only is this thrown out, but God in fact establishes what the convention might regard as evil. Both of these stories clearly establish that God expects human convention to be challenged and provides divine initiatives to ensure that this is done, with conflict as a means for so doing.

## Concluding Comments

We the readers are left to draw conclusions about which of the promises are good and which are evil. The fact is that the text does not lead us to any absolute conclusion, though convention dictates that we think in a certain way. Conflict and strife are almost universally seen as evil. Not surprisingly, many who read and study these texts have continued to adhere to this notion. These parallels suggest otherwise.

### BIBLIOGRAPHY

Brueggemann, Walter
    1982        *Genesis* (Interpretation; Atlanta: John Knox Press).
Janzen, J. Gerald
    1993        *Genesis 12–50: Abraham and All the Families of the Earth* (Grand Rapids: Eerdmans)
Mukherjee, Bharati
    1996        'Genesis (Hagar)', in David Rosenberg (ed.), *Communion: Contemporary Writers Reveal the Bible in Their Lives* (New York: Anchor Books): 89-102.

Pitzele, Peter
    1995        *Our Fathers' Wells: A Personal Encounter with the Myths of Genesis* (San Francisco: HarperCollins).
Rosenberg, David (trans.), and Harold Bloom (interpreter)
    1990        *The Book of J* (New York: Grove Weidenfeld).
Rosenblatt, Naomi H., and Joshua Horwitz
    1995        *Wrestling with Angels: What the First Family of Genesis Teaches Us about our Spiritual Identity, Sexuality, and Personal Relationships* (New York: Delacorte Press).
Steinberg, Naomi
    1993        *Kinship and Marriage in Genesis: A Household Economics Perspective* (Minneapolis: Fortress Press).
Trible, Phyllis
    1984        *Texts of Terror: Literary-Feminist Readings of Biblical Narratives* (Overtures to Biblical Theology; Minneapolis: Fortress Press).
Visotzky, Burton L.
    1996        *The Genesis of Ethics: How the Tormented Family of Genesis Leads Us to Moral Development* (New York: Crown).
Westermann, Claus
    1985        *Genesis 12–36* (trans. John J. Scullion; Minneapolis: Augsburg).

# Diasporic Reading of a Diasporic Text: Identity Politics and Race Relations and the Book of Esther

JEFFREY KAH-JIN KUAN

## Defining Diasporic Reading

In an essay written in 1991, William Safran began with these words:

> In most scholarly discussions of ethnic communities, immigrants, and aliens, and in most treatments of relationships between minorities and majorities, little if any attention has been devoted to diasporas. In the most widely read books on nationalism and ethnonationalism, the phenomenon is not considered worthy of discussion, let alone index entries (1991: 83).

Since then, diaspora discourse has received substantial attention in cultural studies and the social sciences, to the extent that three years later James Clifford was already saying that 'diasporic language appears to be replacing, or at least supplementing, minority discourse' (1994: 311). Today, diaspora language and discourse is quite common, as attested by the proliferation of works in different fields.

Before attempting a definition of diasporic reading, it is necessary to review how diasporas are being defined in recent discussions. Here again the works of Safran and Clifford set the stage. Applying the concept of diaspora to 'expatriate minority communities', Safran defines them as communities that (1) have been dispersed from an original 'center' to two or more 'peripheral' settings; (2) preserve a 'memory, vision, or myth about their original homeland'; (3) believe that they are not or cannot be fully accepted by their host country; (4) consider their ancestral home as their ideal home and a place of eventual return, at the appropriate time;

(5) have a sense of commitment to the maintenance and restoration of their homeland; and (6) maintain a relationship to the homeland to the extent that their communal consciousness and solidarity are shaped by it (1991: 83–84). Safran's definition, helpful though it may be, has not taken into consideration generational differences in diasporic communities. Clearly, his definition fits well with the first generation of diasporic people.[1] Beyond the first generation, however, the sense of attachment to and the desire to return to the homeland at the appropriate time are often not present.[2]

Dissatisfied with Safran's enumeration of the essential features of diasporas, Clifford offers a different approach, dealing instead with what diasporas define themselves against. Thus, he notes that 'diasporas are caught up with and defined against (1) the norms of nation-states and (2) indigenous, and especially autochthonous, claims by "tribal" peoples' (1994: 307).

First, Clifford makes a distinction between diasporic communities and immigrant communities. Using the United States with its assimilationist national ideology as illustration, Clifford refers to communities of European descent as immigrant communities. While these communities may initially experience loss and nostalgia, more often than not it is just a matter of time before they are assimilated and make the transition to ethnic American status. For diasporic communities, assimilation is not possible, in part because of their allegiance and connection to a homeland or a dispersed community located elsewhere and in part because of their experiences of discrimination and expulsion.[3] Nonetheless, in maintaining communities and having homes away from home, diasporas construct alternate 'forms of community consciousness and solidarity that maintain identifications outside the national time/space in order to live inside, with a difference' (p. 308). Such

1.    Within the Jewish Diaspora, Safran's 'ideal type', the issue of the homeland may be diminished outside of traditional religious settings but remains an extensive part of the messianic tradition as well as of the political Zionist movement. I am indebted to my student, Michael Oblath, for this insight.

2.    Here I speak as one who is doubly diasporic. While I do maintain a strong sense of attachment to Malaysia and still harbor a desire to return, such was not my experience in Malaysia vis-à-vis China.

3.    For the Jewish community, such discrimination takes the form of anti-Semitism.

forms of consciousness and solidarity are often in tension with nation-state or assimilationist ideologies.

Clifford's distinction between immigrant and diaspora communities is drawn, unfortunately, along the line of skin color.[4] The problem is not so much the continuing allegiance of the diaspora community to the homeland but its treatment by the host country.[5] The reality is that in the United States people of Asian heritage are often asked the question, 'Where are you from?' with the implication of, 'Where is your homeland?' (San Juan, Jr 1994). Such implication is seldom raised in relation to immigrants of European heritage. Thus, even if a community has adopted the nation-state ideology, the chances are that they would still be regarded as 'others'.

Second, diasporic communities are also in tension with indigenous, and especially autochthonous, claims. Here the issue is one of rootedness and claim to the land, and the question becomes, 'How long does it take for a people to become "indigenous"?' Such tension is obvious in the modern state of Israel. For the Boyarins, however, this tension is framed in terms of a diaspora ideology that is in conflict with and renounces the concept of autochthonous sovereignty, which is seen as a sense of rootedness that excludes others' claims in the land (Boyarin and Boyarin 1993). Speaking against the national and ethnic absolutism of contemporary Zionism, Jonathan Boyarin writes,

> We Jews should recognize the strength that comes from a diversity of communal arrangements and concentrations both among Jews and with our several others. We should recognize that the copresence of those others is not a threat, but rather the condition of our lives (1992: 129).

A distinctive mark of a diaspora community is its biculturalism (or even multiculturalism in some communities). Such a mark car-

---

4.    There are no doubt other variables in other contexts such as, for example, religious affiliations.

5.    This point was sharply brought home to me by a Korean-American student—a nationalized citizen for more than 20 years—who related his own experience in a class, over the course of a semester, where an international student from Germany was also in attendance. In this predominantly white class, it did not take long for the German student to be treated as an 'American', while the Korean-American was constantly referred to as a foreigner.

ries with it promise and pain. From his perspective as a Hispanic
American, Fernando Segovia writes,

> On the one hand, we live in two worlds at one and the same time,
> operating relatively at ease within each world and able to go in and
> out of each in an endless exercise of human and social translation;
> on the other hand, we live in neither of these worlds, regarded
> askance by their respective populations and unable to call either
> world home (1995: 62).

The reality of such a way of life creates a situation where diasporic
people exist as 'permanent strangers' in their present world or
home (where they are viewed as 'the undesirable 'others', the ones
who do not fit'), and as 'permanent aliens' to their former world
or home (a world that is not easy, and most often impossible, to
return to) (pp. 61–65).

Diasporic discourse, therefore, must take seriously the following
issues: (1) the sense of displacement of diaspora communities,
brought about by sociopolitical, socioeconomic, or religiocultural
reasons; (2) memories or myths of the homeland, since diaspora
communities often see themselves as 'a "people" with historical
roots and destinies outside the time/space of the host nation'
(Clifford 1994: 310); (3) the constructed alternate forms of community consciousness, through which the diaspora communities
exist in tension with nation-state or assimilationist ideologies; and
(4) the biculturalism or multiculturalism that defines diasporic
existence.

In biblical scholarship, Fernando Segovia has begun to articu-
late 'a hermeneutics of the diaspora' (1995: 57–73). In his articulation Segovia stresses the importance of contextualization, both
with regard to the context of the biblical texts and the context of
readers and critics. In addition, he advocates intercultural criticism as a reading strategy for such a hermeneutics. Within such a
reading strategy, (1) 'the contextuality and otherness of the text
must be acknowledged, valued, and analyzed'; (2) the reader is to
be regarded as 'socially and culturally conditioned, as an other to
both text and other readers'; and (3) the interaction between text
and reader is to be regarded as 'an unavoidable filtering of the
one world or entity by and through the other, of the text by and
through the reader'.

## Diasporic Experience of Chinese Americans from Southeast Asia[6]

As a Chinese American from Southeast Asia,[7] I belong to a group of Asian Americans whose existential reality is characterized by multiculturalism. We Chinese Americans from Southeast Asia live in the midst of multiple 'worlds'—the 'homeland' of our ancestors in China, our former 'world' in one of the Southeast Asian sovereign states, and our present 'world' in the United States. It is on the basis of our living and 'interacting' with these disparate worlds that our cultural identity is constructed and reconstructed. Stuart Hall, in talking about cultural identity, writes:

> Cultural identity is not a fixed essence at all, lying unchanged outside history and culture. It is not some universal and transcendental spirit inside us on which history has made no fundamental

6. Lisa Lowe has characterized Asian-American culture as 'heterogeneous' in order to highlight the differences among Asian Americans. She notes: 'From the perspective of the majority culture, Asian Americans may very well be constructed as different from, and other than, Euro-Americans. But from the perspectives of Asian Americans, we are perhaps even more different, more diverse, among ourselves' (1991: 27). Even among Chinese Americans, we are not homogeneous.

7. I am a third-generation Chinese Malaysian. My grandparents went to Malaysia from the Fujian province of south China in the 1920s, during a time of political instability in China that saw a new revolution led by the Nationalist Party (Kuomintang) and the Communist Party (Kungch'antang). Like most Chinese immigrants of their time, they saw themselves as transients who were there solely for economic reasons, with every intention of returning to China once they had made enough money and when the political situation returned to normalcy. That they never made the return a reality was due in large part to the prolonged Sino-Japanese War (1937–45) and the civil war that followed between the Nationalist Party and the Communist Party. With the Communist Party securing control of China, the notion of return became even more remote. Nonetheless, I would still often hear my grandparents using the phrase 'returning to China', in the sense that home was China.

My journey to the United States began as a graduate student in search of educational opportunities. Over the last few years, I have begun to make the transition to identifying myself as a first-generation Chinese-Malaysian-American. In making the transition, I am moving from one diasporic experience to a different diasporic experience. In a sense, I am a rediasporized person, a 'doubly' diasporic person.

mark. It is not a fixed origin to which we can make some final and absolute Return… It is always constructed through memory, fantasy, narrative and myth. Cultural identities are the points of identification, the unstable points of identification or suture, which are made, within the discourses of history and culture. Not an essence but a *positioning*. Hence, there is always a politics of identity, a politics of position, which has no absolute guarantee in an unproblematic, transcendental 'law of origin' (1994: 395).

In reference to the Chinese-American situation, Lisa Lowe notes that 'the making of Chinese-American culture—how ethnicity is imagined, practiced, continued—is worked out as much between ourselves and our communities as it is transmitted from one generation to another' (1991: 27). As Chinese Americans from Southeast Asia, we know all too well the promise and pain of our cultural identity. Our identity is multi-hyphenated (for example, I identify myself as a Chinese-Malaysian-American), and each aspect contributes significantly to the construction of who we are. Two words define our identity, hybridity and liminality.

First, ethnically, we are Chinese and most Chinese families in Southeast Asia have consciously maintained the Chinese religio-cultural traditions. Culturally, we are more Southeast Asian than Chinese. Our contexts in Southeast Asia, while not homogeneous, share some common cultural traits.[8] Most of us speak more than one language—at the very least, a Southeast Asian language and Mandarin Chinese or a dialect, but most often also the language of our colonizers, be it English, Dutch, French or Spanish. Given our new 'permanent home' in the United States, we are also becoming in practice 'Americanized'. This kind of cultural identity is 'highly hybridized'. This hybridity may be viewed positively in that we are able to negotiate our way from one world to another quite effortlessly, because in a sense we live in all different worlds at the same time.[9] Our hybridity also puts us in a position to be an interpreter of each of the different worlds we move in and out of on a daily basis.

---

8.   For example, it is only in Southeast Asia that we eat with fork and spoon!

9.   In fact, it may be more accurate to say that all the different worlds 'live' in us at the same time.

Second, because of our hybrid cultural identity, our existence is marked also by liminality, a state of 'in-betweenness'. Fumitaka Matsuoka, in talking about the liminal world in which many Asian Americans find ourselves, describes it as follows:

> It is at once the world of isolation and intimacy, desolation and creativity. A person in a liminal world is poised in uncertainty and ambiguity between two or more social constructs, reflecting in the soul the discords and harmonies, repulsions and attractions. One of the constructs is likely to be dominant, whether cultural or linguistic. Within such a dominant construct one strives to belong and yet finds oneself to be a peripheral member, forced to remain in the world of in-betweenness (1995: 54).

A liminal state is an existential reality for Chinese Americans from Southeast Asia. We have learned how to exist in such a state even in our former host country. For most of us, we were never completely embraced by our host country. We could never fully become Malaysian, Burmese, Indonesian, and so forth, because the host country would always define us as 'the Chinese in our midst'. We were 'wanted' as long as we could contribute to the economic wellbeing of our host country, and 'unwanted' as soon as problems arose.[10] Our response to our host country, therefore, was not surprisingly marked by uncertainty, ambiguity and caution. Our liminality is magnified as we settle into a new host country. We have no expectation of being fully embraced by the dominant society in America. We must know how to live in a world of in-betweenness and must know how to thrive in it, culturally, linguistically and economically.

Such then is the nature of our diasporic community. We have 'worlds' that we live in, but not a place we can call 'home'. We are highly hybridized and live in a state of utter liminality. By inscribing our identity, we remove the power of the dominant society to inscribe us.

## Reading Esther from a Diasporic Perspective

It is from such a diasporic lens that I read the book of Esther. That the book of Esther is a literary product of a diaspora Jewish

10. The treatment of Chinese Indonesians is a classic example, with its

community is certain. Many modern commentators would date the book in the Hellenistic period, either in the fourth or third century BCE.[11] What is the genre of the book? In his survey of the history of interpretation regarding the generic classification of the book, Michael Fox lists seven such possibilities: wisdom literature; Persian chronicle; historical novella or romance; diaspora story; history; festival etiology; festival lection (1991: 142-51). In the following I want to argue that the book is a 'diaspora novella' (Humphreys 1973; Meinhold 1975, 1976), written as a means to inscribe Jewish cultural identity in the diaspora. I will illustrate this by using three texts from the book.

*Esther 2.5-10*
The first text is Est. 2.5-10. As the story goes, King Ahasuerus throws a lavish party for all the people in the citadel of Susa. At the same time, Queen Vashti also gives a banquet for the women. On the seventh day, the king commands the queen to appear in order that he may show her off before the people. When the queen refuses, the king is advised to depose her and 'give her royal position to another who is better than she' (1.19). Thus begins the search for Vashti's replacement. The text then introduces the two main characters, Esther and Mordecai.

Mordecai is introduced as follows:

> There was a Jew in the citadel of Susa whose name was Mordecai ben Jair ben Shimei ben Kish, a Benjaminite, who was exiled from Jerusalem with the exiles who were exiled with Jeconiah, king of Judah, whom Nebuchadnezzar, king of Babylon had exiled (2.5-6).

Two things stand out in this introduction: identity and displacement of the character.

His identity is convoluted. On the one hand, he is clearly regarded as a 'citizen' of Susa, bearing a non-Hebrew name. On the other hand, the narrator goes to great length to inscribe Mordecai as an 'other'. His patronym is three generations long, with Hebrew

pattern of using the Chinese-Indonesian population as scapegoat in times of socioeconomic crisis.

11. The book's *terminus a quo* is usually set as the fourth century BCE, while its *terminus ad quem* is fixed as 94 CE, the date of Josephus's *Antiquities*, in which he retold the story of Esther. Between these termini, a variety of dates have been suggested (see Moore 1992: 641).

names that call to mind the monarchical tradition.[12] He is a 'Jew' (*'iš yᵉhûdî*) and a Benjaminite (*'iš yᵉmînî*), identifiers that are tribal, cultural and political. While the term relates *'iš yᵉhûdî* to his Jewishness, a religiocultural identification, it can refer also to his Judean origin, a political identification. He is in a sense introduced as a multihyphenated character, a 'Benjaminite-Judean/Jewish-"Persian"'. As such, Mordecai's cultural identity is 'highly hybridized',[13] each aspect contributing significantly to the construction of his identity and, more importantly, to the identity of his diasporic community. As a hybridized people, the diasporic community of Mordecai, therefore, lives and travels back and forth among several 'worlds' at the same time and is an interpreter of one culture to the other. As hybrids, however, they never belong to any of the worlds they live in, and, as a result of such a constructed identity, there is no one place to return to.

The construction of this kind of identity is closely related to the experience of 'displacement'. The significance of this experience in shaping the cultural consciousness of the diaspora Jewish community is highlighted by the four appearances of the word *gālâ* in v. 6: 'who was *exiled* from Jerusalem with the *exiles* who were *exiled* with Jeconiah, king of Judah, whom Nebuchadnezzar, king of Babylon had *exiled*'. This is a verbose way to make a point, but it seeks to emphasize how important the experience is. The relative particle *'ᵃšer* that begins the verse makes it ambiguous about who was taken into exile, Mordecai or his great-grandfather. That point is moot. The repetition of the term emphasizes that it is the experience of displacement itself that is significant.

The introduction of the next character, Esther, complicates the issue of identity construction. Esther is introduced by way of her relationship to Mordecai:

> He was raising Hadassah, that is, Esther, the daughter of his uncle, for she had no father or mother. The young woman was beautiful in appearance and pleasing to look at. When her father and mother died, Mordecai took her as his daughter (2.7).

12. On the intertextual nature of the patronym, see Beal (1997: 33).

13. Beal notes that 'at this initial introduction of the first Jewish character in the narrative, his very title suggests ambiguity in Jewish identity' (1997: 33).

In contrast to Mordecai, Esther has both a Hebrew and a non-Hebrew name, magnifying the two worlds in which she has to negotiate her way. The story goes on to relate that she, along with other beautiful women, is drafted into the beauty pageant designed to find a new consort for the king. In the midst of that, 'Esther did not mention her people and her kindred, for Mordecai had commanded her not to mention it' (2.10). Thus, at this stage, Jewish identity is suppressed and Esther is presented as being undifferentiatable from the other ethnic groups. As Esther she is embraced as a 'Persian', a subject of the Empire like all other subjects. At one level, then, the process of assimilation to the host country is successful. She has a place where she belongs.

This lack of differentiation of the Jews in the midst of other peoples is bolstered by 3.4, where Mordecai has to tell others that 'he was a Jew' before his ethnicity can be identified. The diaspora Jewish community in that sense has learned to fit into the world of their host country. Segovia's description of the Hispanic-American diaspora can be applied aptly to the ancient Jewish context, in that they know how to operate 'relatively at ease within each world and able to go in and out of each in an endless exercise of human and social translation' (1995: 62). Knowing how to fit in and what the royal protocol is eventually won for Esther the crown of Vashti.

*Esther 3*
The second text is Esther 3. If ch. 2 is about the hybridity of the diaspora Jewish community, ch. 3 highlights its liminality. If ch. 2 ends with a sense of 'wantedness' on the part of the Jewish community,[14] ch. 3 sees the situation quickly evaporating and turning into one of 'unwantedness'. Here we find Haman the Agagite seeking to destroy the Jews. This is the ambiguity and uncertainty that mark life in the diaspora. In this liminal state, a diaspora community can never predict how it will be responded to and treated by the other people of the society. The diaspora community always sits on the edge of promise and pain.

What brings about this liminal state for the Jewish community? Earlier, I noted that Clifford defines diaspora against the norm of nation-states. He further suggests that a diaspora community

---

14. Mordecai's discovery of a plot to assassinate the king scores points for the Jewish community and enhances the feeling of 'wantedness' by the Jews.

oftentimes constructs alternate 'forms of community consciousness and solidarity that maintain identifications outside the national time/space in order to live inside, with a difference' (1994:
308). This 'over-againstness' is made clear in ch. 3, where Haman
says to the king: 'One people diverge, scattered and separated
among the peoples in all the provinces of your kingdom; their
laws are different from every other people and they do not keep
the laws of the king' (3.8). Framed in the form of Haman's
accusation, it is possible to maintain that in the diaspora the Jewish
community was not willing to subscribe to the national ideology of
the host country (*dātē hammelek*), but rather maintained its own
laws (*datîm*). Thus, the diasporic Jews constructed for themselves
an alternate form of community consciousness different from
every other people whereby they maintained their difference. The
community constructed a politics of identity in order that its
members' religiocultural identity not be eroded and in order for
them to live in two or more worlds at one and the same time. The
diaspora Jewish community, like other diaspora communities, in
so doing remains an 'other'.[15]

## Esther 9

Finally, I move to ch. 9, the most difficult part of the book of
Esther, a text that speaks about the annihilation of their enemies
by the Jews. It is a senseless act of violence from an ethical perspective. David Clines is correct to note that the narrator is here
presenting a massacre of anti-Semites rather than a battle of self-
defense against a royally supported pogrom (1984: 40). Clines is
wrong, however, when he considers chs. 9 and 10 as unrelated
originally to chs. 1–8 (1984: 29–30).[16] From the perspective of the
book of Esther as a 'diaspora novella' and of the text as a construction of Jewish identity in the diaspora, ending up with such a
text does make sense. This chapter can be seen as part of a strategy of survival, as well as a strategy of resistance to complete assimilation, brought about by a history of discrimination and oppres-

15. 'Otherness', Segovia argues, does have a positive dimension (1995:
65-67).

16. Kenneth Craig argues, from the perspective of a 'literary carnivalesque
tradition', that Est. 9 is an integral part of the story (1995: 135-36).

sion. Clifford has noted that 'some of the most violent articulations of purity and racial exclusivism come from diaspora populations. Such discourses are usually weapons of the (relatively) weak' (1994: 307). Again, such discourse reflects the complexity of constructing cultural identity in a diaspora. Because diaspora communities live in a world of isolation and intimacy, alienation and embrace, it is only natural that such a story about eliminating the oppressors and alienators would be utilize to create community identity.

## Concluding Comment

In conclusion, diasporic discourse helps to illuminate some of the features in both the language and the narrative in the book of Esther and aids us in appreciating Esther as a 'diaspora novella' and as a form of the construction of cultural identity.

BIBLIOGRAPHY

Beal, Timothy K.
  1997          *The Book of Hiding: Gender, Ethnicity, Annihilation, and Esther* (London: Routledge).
Boyarin, Jonathan
  1992          *Storm from Paradise: The Politics of Jewish Memory* (Minneapolis: University of Minnesota Press).
Boyarin, Daniel, and Jonathan Boyarin
  1993          'Diaspora: Generational Ground of Jewish Identity', *Critical Inquiry* 19: 693-725.
Clifford, James
  1994          'Diasporas', *Cultural Anthropology* 9: 302-38.
Clines, David J.A.
  1984          *The Esther Scroll: The Story of a Story* (JSOTSup, 30; Sheffield: JSOT Press).
Craig, Kenneth
  1995          *Reading Esther: A Case for the Literary Carnivalesque* (Louisville, KY: Westminster/John Knox Press).

Fox, Michael V.
  1991          *Character and Ideology in the Book of Esther* (Columbia: University of South Carolina Press).
Hall, Stuart
  1994          'Cultural Identity and Diaspora', in P. Williams and L. Chrisman (eds.), *Colonial Discourse and Post-Colonial Theory: A Reader* (New York: Columbia University Press): 392-403.

Humphreys, W. Lee
   1973        'A Life-style for Diaspora: A Study of the Tales of Esther and Daniel', *Journal of Biblical Literature* 92: 211-23.

Lowe, Lisa
   1991        'Heterogeneity, Hybridity, Multiplicity: Marking Asian American Differences', *Diaspora* 1: 24-44.

Matsuoka, Fumitaka
   1995        *Out of Silence: Emerging Themes in Asian American Churches* (Cleveland: United Church Press).

Meinhold, Arndt
   1975        'Die Gattung der Josephgeschichte und des Estherbuches: Diaspora-novelle. Part I', *Zeitschrift für die alttestamentliche Wissenschaft* 87: 306-24.
   1976        'Die Gattung der Josephgeschichte und des Estherbuches: Diaspora-novelle. Part II', *Zeitschrift für die alttestamentliche Wissenschaft* 88: 72-93.

Moore, Carey A.
   1992        'Esther, Book of', in D.N. Freedman (ed.), *The Anchor Bible Dictionary* (6 vols.; New York: Doubleday): II, 633-43.

Safran, William
   1991        'Diasporas in Modern Societies: Myths of Homeland and Return', *Diaspora* 1: 83-99.

San Juan, E., Jr
   1994        'The Predicament of Filipinos in the United States: "Where Are You From? When Are You Going Back?"', in K. Aguilar-San Juan (ed.), *The State of Asian America: Activism and Resistance in the 1990s* (Boston: South End Press): 205-18.

Segovia, Fernando F.
   1995        'Toward a Hermeneutics of the Diaspora: A Hermeneutics of Otherness and Engagement', in F.F. Segovia and M.A. Tolbert (eds.), *Reading from This Place*. I. *Social Location and Biblical Interpretation in the United States* (Minneapolis: Fortress Press): 57-73.

# Hermeneutics of the Bible and 'Cricket as Text': Reading as an Exile

I realize that the task I have set myself has placed me on a 'sticky wicket' and that the expected difficulty I have encountered in thinking about and writing this essay has often left me stranded 'outside the crease'. Whether I am 'stumped' on account of the approach I take, I leave it up to you, the other players—the readers. In this essay I will attempt to show how the game of cricket is a 'text' that has informed and interpreted and continues to inform and interpret the life of the people of the English-speaking Caribbean. The 'text' of cricket provides the fabric for sociocultural, ethnic and religious integration as well as survival in a world that is considered alien, unpredictable and unequal. Cricket is a 'common' text that serves to unite the various peoples of the English-speaking Caribbean across ethnic, religious, economic and cultural boundaries. In this world, the Bible, in both the private and public spheres, remains the primary religious text, while Hindu texts and the Koran also play the central role for Hindus and Muslims, respectively, who are mainly descendants of East Indian emigrants from the Indian sub-continent. In some countries, such as Trinidad, there are groups of Black Muslims.

Over the last three decades or so, emigration from the Caribbean (and the southern hemisphere) has reached very high proportions, with peoples of all ethnic, religious and class groupings leaving for a 'better life'. It has been observed that many who have physically emigrated have never fully left 'home', even as they pursue the 'better life' for themselves and for their children. They—and, for many, their children as well—experience discontinuity and continuity, exile and 'at homeness' in their new country.

Many carry within themselves, at the very core of their being, more often than not in submerged ways, the paradoxical sense of 'home' as both the new land where they now live and the old land from which they have come. They reject any suggestion that belonging to the 'new home' means cutting off the ties—of family, culture, religion, ethnicity, and so forth—with the 'old home'. Equally, they insist that ties to the 'new home' should not mean rejection by those who remain behind in the 'old home'.

I will attend to this phenomenon with special, though not exclusive, reference to the East Indian community in the English-speaking Caribbean. As the topic of this essay indicates, the focus will be on how cricket has functioned as a liberating 'text' that has served to interpret the lives of the East Indian community in particular and Caribbean people as a whole. From this investigation, I will attempt some hermeneutical 'shots' that may be played with respect to interpreting biblical texts on exile, specifically the book of Ruth, which, for the purpose of the argument in this essay, I have assumed is a postexilic writing.[1]

## Cricket as Text

My approach is an attempt to take up the challenge issued by C.L.R. James when he criticizes Neville Cardus, one of the finest cricket writers of the twentieth century, for not going beyond introducing 'music into his cricket writing' to introducing 'cricket into his writing on music'. James concludes:

> Cardus is a victim of that categorization and specialization, that division of the human personality, which is the greatest curse of our time. Cricket has suffered, but not only cricket. The aestheticians have scorned to take notice of popular sports and games—to their own detriment. The aridity and confusion of which they so mournfully complain will continue until they include organized games *and the people who watch them* as an integral part of their data.

James is convinced that 'cricket is an art, not a bastard or poor relation, but a full member of the community... Cricket is first and foremost a dramatic spectacle. It belongs with the theatre, ballet, opera and the dance' (1969: 191-92).

---

1.  For a summary of scholarly positions on the date of writing, see Hamlin (1996: 12) and Hubbard (1988: 24-35).

From the early nineteenth century, when cricket was introduced in the West Indies, to today, widespread critical notice was taken of those who took to the field, who took up what positions, and who was the captain. That critical notice has increased rather than declined over the years. Those factors were primary indicators of power and authority, subservience and deference. As J.S. Barker tells us, 'West Indian cricket was exclusively a White Man's game, until well into the second half of the century' (1967: 7; see esp. Beckles 1994: xiii).

Every cricket match where the colonial pride of the West Indies was at stake was an occasion in which fractured, bruised, unclear, dual and multiple identities were enhanced, dismissed or even created afresh (Birbalsingh 1996: 15). C.L.R. James, the quintessential cricket analyst of West Indian life and one of the best cricket interpreters of the twentieth century, insightfully observes, 'The intimate connection between cricket and West Indian social and political life was established so that all except the wilfully perverse could see' (1969: 217). It does not matter whether all West Indians play (or have played) the game and/or follow it; the basic point is that cricket is a—some may say 'the'—primary text, unwritten and written, that interprets their lives. James insightfully writes:

> What do they know of cricket who only cricket know? West Indians crowding to tests bring with them the whole past history and future hopes of the islands. English people, for example, have a conception of themselves breathed from birth. Drake and mighty Nelson, Shakespeare, Waterloo, the Charge of the Light Brigade, the few who did so much for so many, the success of parliamentary democracy, those and such as those constitute a national tradition. Underdeveloped countries have to go back centuries to rebuild one. We of the West Indies have none at all, none that we know of. To such people the three W's, Ram and Val wrecking English batting, help to fill a huge gap in their consciousness and in their needs (1969: 225).[2]

Cricket was introduced into the Caribbean by the British elite solely for their pleasure (Barker 1967: 7). Only those with the power to determine the time of work, rest and leisure could intro-

---

2.   See James's later (1963) and emended version of this observation, where he adds, 'the front-page scoring of cricketers like Garfield Sobers and Rohan Kanhai fill[s] gnawing gaps in their consciousness and in their needs' (1986: 124).

duce a game or activity for their own pleasure and that of the select few. All others, at best, could be spectators who derive pleasure from singling out particular players for their unsolicited support and appreciation (Sobers 1967: 51). Of course, despite their distance from the small elite who played, many of the masses came to identify with a team, more often than not their own 'local' team.

When people observe from the margin, as the Caribbean masses did, arguably until the 1950s, they act out of their imposed and internalized identity. 'Know your place' was the hallmark of the dynamic of their identity. Even when Coloureds and Blacks began to play the game, they played from the margin, from the boundary, not in the 'middle' or 'centre'. In theory, once they were picked for the team and thereby allowed on the field, 'the sacred space' (Beckles 1994: xvi), the rules applied equally to all the players—skill, not ascriptive rights, determined their place in the team at play. In other words, they, too, played in the 'middle'. This point will be crucial when we make the hermeneutical leap to Ruth the Moabite, who chooses to find refuge under the wings of Yahweh (2.12).

Not every nation that plays cricket views the game in the same way as West Indians do. Allen Guttmann accurately observes, 'We can learn a great deal from careful attention to the games a society emphasizes, but the "same" game is likely to vary greatly in its meaning from one cultural context to another' (1978: 11). In this vein, Frank Birbalsingh, writing on 'Westindian' cricket, poignantly summarizes:

> Cricket plays a special role in the historical, social and cultural development of the English-speaking Caribbean. It is not like hockey in Canada, baseball in the United States, or even cricket in England. In the English-speaking Caribbean, cricket does not merely stimulate delight or devotion; it is like the bull fight in Spain: a spectacle that can galvanize a people's spiritual resources, stimulate their national self-esteem, remind them of their place in the world. Defensive-minded people will think that this view of cricket demeans Westindians. On the contrary, it recognizes Westindian resistance to an oppressive colonial legacy; *for it acknowledges Test cricket as the first opportunity that Westindians had of demonstrating their abilities on the international scene.* [Emphasis added.] This is not to underplay the achievements of great Westindians such as Captain Cipriani, Hubert Nathaniel Critchlow, and Marcus Garvey in advancing the social, political, and cultural development of the region. Nor does it

suggest that Westindians can only demonstrate excellence in sport, any more than it suggests that Spaniards can only fight bulls. The fact is that the performance of Westindian cricketers, since 1928, has achieved the widest recognition for territories such as Trinidad, Jamaica, Barbados, and Guyana [and Antigua and the Leeward and Windward Islands], especially among ordinary people in the English-speaking world outside of the United States (1988: 15).[3]

Birbalsingh concludes his essay by reiterating his emphasis 'that cricket is not merely a game in the Westindies'. Birbalsingh attempts to show the 'Caribbeanness' of the Indo-Caribbean players 'who have successfully broken out from the shared colonial oppression of slavery/indenture to express an impulse for freedom that is universal' (p. 25).

When, as in the history of the English-speaking Caribbean, the occasional rebellion, not revolution, was the only option for expression of the impulse for freedom, then entering the masters' domain of play and leisure and mastering it from within, with all the attendant feelings of inferiority or superiority, provide a psychological victory that, though ephemeral, lasts longer than the duration of the event and reaches beyond those who play the game or follow it with consistent enthusiasm. In other words, 'cricket as text' gives the oppressed a vital reason for believing that they are not what they seem—marginalized, powerless, essentially inferior beings. And 'home' is precisely where they experience such systemic, existential ignominy. Through the 'test' of cricket, they come to realize and believe that in the inner recesses of their being there are truly genius and creativity that await opportunity for expression and celebration. 'Carnival' or 'calypso' cricket may miss the point of the whole experience of survival and inner (and outer material) development. Yet, understood as genuine celebration, such 'calypso' or 'carnival' cricket bespeaks the eruption of a new identity of creativity, freedom and possibilities (Beckles 1994; Beckles and Stoddart 1995).

To get at the themes of dual and multiple identities and the meaning of exile, it is instructive to evaluate the career of the

3.    This work came out in 1988, the year marking the 150th anniversary of the arrival of the first group of indentured emigrants from India to Guyana, in May 1838. It is accurately noted on the back cover, 'This is more than a book about Indo-Westindian cricket. It is a privileged journey into the soul of the Indo-Westindians'.

most celebrated Indo-West Indian cricketer to date: Rohan Babulal Kanhai, whose career began in the mid-1950s and saw the collapse, in Guyana, in 1955, of 'the fragile coalition across the racial chasm' (Shiwcharan 1988: 59). More than any other ethnic group in Guyana and Trinidad, East Indians, the newest comers to the sugar plantations, were immigrants who, until about 1955, could return to India as Indian citizens. In the eyes of the others in the society, especially the Afro-Guyanese, East Indians' identification with their new 'home' in the Caribbean was therefore suspect.[4] East Indians had increased the diversity in the Caribbean—especially Guyana and Trinidad—by bringing with them their Hindu and Islamic religions, their sense of caste distinctions, their languages and their preference for the lighter-complexioned among them. They were not White Europeans nor were they Africans. Especially to the Afro-Guyanese, they had not yet 'arrived'![5]

Within themselves, Shiwcharan points out, there was 'a nagging, trying doubt'. National politics offered one concrete though tenuous place to erase such doubt. The other concrete and tenuous place to erase such doubt and acquire some sense of dignity as a group was through cricket. Indo-Guyanese had come to the realization that 'cricket as text' was a primary text to be interpreted from within. If one or more of them could distinguish themselves in the game, then there was the possibility for esteem and recognition beyond their own group. Shiwcharan writes:

> We felt that we had not arrived in the estimation of Afro-Guyanese. The political victory, economic and professional advances, were all quite impressive. And the possibilities were seemingly endless. But to produce a great Westindian batsman—that was the ultimate test; for no other person, not even a nobel laureate in physics or medicine, calls up in the black Westindian such a torrent of spontaneous joy, dignity and high communion as a batsman of genius. That was what we hoped for, prayed for, talked about and dreamt in the late 50s—that Kanhai would not let us down.
>
> We felt that he was sent to us with a mission to erase that yawning deficiency with excellence, and that if he did not succeed, a massive shame would descend upon us... I suspect that this haunt-

---

4. This sense of unclarity and ambiguity in how East Indians perceived themselves is well presented in Roy Heath's novel, *The Shadow Bride* (1988).

5. Naipaul's use of the term 'the enigma of arrival' in relation to his own arrival in England is a fitting description here (1987).

ing messianic challenge nourished his art, and released and sharp-
ened the excellence (1988: 59).

Writing in the same vein as James, who posed the question,
'What do they know of cricket who only cricket know?' Shiwcharan, too, is 'concerned to place cricket on a map of human
activities' (Brearley 1969: 10). For the Indo-Guyanese community,
the West Indies tour of India in 1958–59, which included two
Indo-Guyanese, Rohan Kanhai and Joe Solomon, was not only
about cricket. 'Kanhai's going to India', Shiwcharan writes, 'was
loaded with deep symbolic and psychological meanings' (1988:
60). Setting the tour to India in the context of the ambivalent
feelings that the Indo-Guyanese community had for India, Shiwcharan soberingly points out:

> Kanhai's tour became a sort of allegorical journey for us all. A sense
> of homecoming prevailed; and we could not countenance being
> less than supreme. Anything less would suggest a squandering of
> the years, a real loss of caste. We yearned to conquer; yet we wished
> to belong (1988: 60-61).

Kanhai's performances in the first two test matches against India
were average at best, due mainly to the guile of the Indian world-
class leg-spinner, Subhash Gupte. It was the same Gupte who, in
1953, having mesmerized the West Indian batsmen, had become a
hero to Indo-Guyanese. The identification with Gupte and the
sense of worth that his splendid performance inspired in the Indo-
Guyanese community was shortlived and was replaced with the
more basic sense of insecurity and uncertainty as to who they
were. As Shiwcharan poignantly says, 'But with Kanhai seemingly a
possession of Gupte, to us this now inspired shame, a reassertion
of patriarchal authority, snuffing out tentative autonomy and em-
bryonic independence. We felt depleted and cowered' (1988: 61).

The drama was greatly heightened when the third test match was
played in Calcutta, from whose port the majority of the 'bound
coolies' had departed for the West Indies during the period 1838–
1917. 'For us, Calcutta was India' (p. 63). On New Year's Day,
1959, Kanhai played a most remarkable innings of 256 runs, still
the highest test score against India, in India, by a West Indian
batsman. That was the gift of newfound identity to a people who
were not disgraced in leaving 'home'. They had scaled new heights.
Shiwcharan says it well: '[T]o my innocent eyes, but maturing

mind, I discerned that the conquest of India was an event in our lives, not just a score to be appreciated for a day' (1988: 62).

The meaning of Kanhai's innings of conquest was more than an intra-Indian affair. It extended to the meaning of the Indo-Caribbean people's Caribbeanness. Noting the multifaceted significance of Kanhai's conquest in the 'middle', Shiwcharan writes:

> For some, Kanhai's conquest at Calcutta was a private thing. The loss attendant upon the crossing of the 'Kala pani', the humiliation of the returnees in their home villages, fed a poignant sense of loss, a deep hurt, and an ambivalence towards India. Several returnees had returned to Guyana, broken, dejected people. Kanhai's mastery over India represented an assertion of the exile's repossession of himself, a reconstituted self, and a triumph over the pretentious, cruel rigidities of the homeland and its dubious obsessions with purity and cant. It was an absolution.
>
> Kanhai's supremacy at Calcutta recalled the Calcutta of the depot, the place where the recently-recruited indentureds were corralled, awaiting embarkation for Demerara. Calcutta had become a metaphor for dislocation, separation, and the loss of traditional certainties, however inhibiting. Calcutta was evocative of layers of private, symbolic associations of negation. But it had a collective resonance. And this Calcutta victory by this returning grandson represented a negation of this negation—a reconstitution of the splintered psyche, an erasure of the nagging ambivalence and the stubborn incoherence of the Diaspora. It symbolized a repossession of an integrated ancestral totality, however deceptive; an appropriation of an ancestral essence to stem a perceived receding Indianness, something over which we agonized, but were unable to stop. Kanhai had brought back the fire; and it wasn't stolen.
>
> The epic at Calcutta had its Caribbean meaning as well. The character of Kanhai's innings, suffused with the authentic Westindian spirit of joy and rhythm, had earned for the Indo-Guyanese the right to be taken seriously: Kanhai was a Westindian man, and with his Indianness reaffirmed, he could confront the Caribbean reality with a new self-confidence. The Indian, ground down by physical complexes about his supposedly weak, effeminate body, could now affect a greater confidence in his body through the athleticism of Kanhai, the man's amazing speed between wickets, his gift of rhythm and aesthetic abandon, his Herculean stamina. The epic at Calcutta erased the deep hurt, the image of the cringing coolie, with the frail, supine body. Kanhai, indeed, was not just king for a day; he was enthroned with the pantheon of the Hindu Gods (1988: 63).

The communal identification with Kanhai's exploits on the cricket field did not begin and end with his majestic performances against India. Against the English, the Australians and the Pakistanis, his performances continued to draw people to cricket as a text that interpreted our lives. One illustration from the West Indies tour of Australia, 1960–61, is instructive. The significance of playing against White people and being watched and positively evaluated by them in their own backyard was ever before us, both the players and masses. On that tour Kanhai emerged as the best batsman in the world, and he was compared to the legendary Australian batsman, Sir Donald Bradman. Shiwcharan correctly observes that during the 1960–61 series, 'when white people in Australia abandoned themselves to the man's mastery, we all felt we were somebody', we felt 'that we mattered' (1988: 67). That included our mothers, sisters...our women folk, most of whom literally had no time for cricket. With humour and insight, Shiwcharan reminisces:

> I grew up among these Hindu deities and their bizarre visual representations. I could not ignore them; I could not be neutral. I was awed into fantasy. Many nights during the Australian tour in 1961, I would lie in bed thinking of Kanhai flat on his back as the ball disappeared among white people, and I would try to will myself to sleep. But a strange fantasy would intrude, and I would see Kanhai on a winged chariot moving in the sky, decorated with stars, like in the pictures of Hindu deities on our wall.
>
> I did not mount Kanhai's pictures among my mother's deities; she would have uprooted them. I collected cuttings and pictures and filed them. So Mom never sprinkled holy water on Kanhai. But one night in January 1961, when he was approaching his second century in the Adelaide Test, she got up and, in her negative way, asked, "E out a ready, nuh?', I replied, 'Yu mad or wah? 'e about fu mek 'e second hundred. Hear.' She sucked her teeth in that peculiarly Westindian way: 'Me mus' 'e get time. Jis now 'e ga out.' She stayed around, pretending to do something or the other. It was her way of concealing that it mattered very much to her how Kanhai did. But she was listening. A solid tension hung in the air as Kanhai got into the 90s; the odd remark was forced. But the century was made; we were all ecstatic, save Mom. When things had subsided, I stole a glance at her, and for one fleeting moment I saw her wipe a tear from her eye. She walked away. I suspect she saw that I also could not restrain myself. I went to bed, and for several hours

afterwards, I could not sleep. I thought hard. But I could not make sense of these things. Not then (1988: 67-68).

## Reading Ruth

The question I must ponder now is, 'How does "cricket as text" help in my reading and interpretation of the book of Ruth?' In becoming the wife of one of Naomi's sons, she a Moabite woman and he an Israelite, she had been allowed within the 'boundary'. While she initially 'played' closer to the 'boundary' than 'the middle', that was not the primary playing position she occupied. Eventually, Ruth the 'foreigner' became a symbol of courage and inclusiveness, even to the 'exiled' people of Israel who had to come to grips with their new 'home'! I turn now to a literary analysis of some of the specifics of the story.

The time has come for the Israelite widow Naomi to return home to Judah, after her experience of life and death as a sojourner in Moab. In the face of the famine in Judah, Moab has been life-sustaining for her household, which included her husband, Elimelech, and their two sons, Mahlon and Chilion. The sons have even found suitable Moabite wives, Ruth and Orpah, who consequently serve Yahweh instead of the gods of Moab. Naomi has also experienced profound grief on the death of her husband, and later of their two sons. Now word has come that the famine has ended in Judah, and so Naomi decides that it is time to return home alone. Despite Naomi's insistence to her daughters-in-law, 'Go back each of you to your mother's house' (1.8), Ruth refuses to comply with Naomi's urging to go back 'to her people and to her gods' (1.15).

Already in her defiance she begins to redefine how she would play the game of partnering Naomi. She changes the rules, not by remaining outside the house of Naomi but precisely by choosing to live within it, with all the consequent responsibilities and challenges. At one fundamental level, when we consider the question of dual identity of the characters in the story, it is Naomi and Elimelech and their sons who have such an identity. Naomi lives in the 'in-betweenness' of being an Ephrathite who follows the way of Yahweh in Moab and who returns to Bethlehem as an erstwhile sojourner in Moab. It is clear that in Judah, then in Moab, and back again in Judah, Naomi is faithful to Yahweh. She has a claim on Judah, and vice versa. She identifies herself with the people of the Lord who 'had considered his people and given them food' (1.6). Even when she complains that 'the Almighty has dealt bitterly with me', noting that she had gone away 'full, but the Lord has brought me back empty', she does not turn away from Yahweh. In the face of the harsh treatment that she bitterly declares she has received from Yahweh, she does not respond by turning to the gods of Moab. Indeed, it is Ruth and Orpah who turn to Yahweh, and it is Ruth who insists that Naomi's house, her future, and her God will be hers as well. Despite Naomi's bitterness toward God, Ruth insists on her right to her new identity in Naomi's household. Having been included in the world of Divine chosenness through marriage, even death and the bitterness of her widowed mother-in-law will not remove nor diminish Ruth's resolve to let Naomi's future be hers, and vice versa.

Ruth seemingly turns her back on her Moabite background, even though the common way in which she is almost consistently identified throughout the story is as 'the Moabite' 'from the country of Moab' (1.22; 2.2, 6, 21; 4.5, 10). She never identifies herself as a Moabite or as coming from Moab, except that she refers to herself as a foreigner in her early exchange with Boaz (2.10), and later, at the threshing floor with Boaz, she tells him, 'I am Ruth, your servant' (3.9; cf. 2.13, where she says to him, '…I am not one of your servants').

It is instructive that her loyalty (*hesed*, 1.8; 2.20; 3.10; see Hamlin 1996: 16-17; Hubbard 1988: 65-66, 72-74) to Naomi, which Boaz and the people publicly applaud, singles her out as exemplifying the kind of loyalty to Yahweh that a faithful Israelite should display. Here, the foreigner in Israel shows that she is paradoxically not a foreigner to Yahweh's expectations of covenant loyalty. Having begun just within the 'boundary of play', she easily and gracefully moves to the 'middle', to the centre, where her conduct is exemplary, as if to the manner born. She re-defines who really is *hesed* in the game or drama of covenant *hesed*, opening up the possibility that Israel will learn about who they are as a people by learning to play the game like Ruth the Moabite. Quite literally, the foreigner to Israel and Israel's God teaches Israel about Yahweh's *hesed* and their consequent *hesed* to Yahweh, to one another, and to the foreigner. In her first encounter with Boaz, his unexpected kindness to her is so overwhelming that 'she fell prostrate, with her face to the ground, and said to him, "Why have I found favor in your sight, that you should take notice of me, when I am a foreigner?"' His answer is instructive:

> All that you have done for your mother-in-law since the death of your husband has been fully told me, and how you left your father and mother and your native land and came to a people that you did not know before (2.10-11).

Once given the opportunity to live in Naomi's house, Ruth never looks back to what she has given up. The reader is left to ponder long the question of the continuity of her new identity as a faithful member of Yahweh's covenant people and her past as one who worshipped the gods of Moab. In a curious way, it may be conjectured, if we place the most positive consequence upon Orpah's return to Moab, it is Orpah who must now live as an exile with the dual identity of one blessed by Yahweh and one who has a new Moabite husband with whom she follows the gods of Moab. Orpah's turning back is not characterized as one of shame and apostasy. Naomi speaks matter-of-factly about her returning to 'her gods' (1.15).

We learn nothing about Ruth's persistent loyalty to Moab; indeed, in choosing to go with Naomi, she redefines who her people will be—those of the covenant with Yahweh (Trible 1978: 173). Does not Ruth's act of clinging to Naomi (1.14) signal her total abandonment of her mother's house and Moab's gods (Chemosh) and her ties to the 'old' land, its people and its culture? (Hubbard 1988: 115-20). The unequivocal 'yes' does not put an end to the question of whether in a fundamental way her new identity is not in fact dual. Arguably, it is Orpah who has the burden of responsibility to point her people to the way of Yahweh, which she would have learnt in the household of Naomi. But we are unable to pursue this question on the basis of the text.

Boaz begins in the 'middle'. Nothing is said about his ancestral and economic background. The very first time he appears in the story, he is described as a person of wealth and substance: 'Now Naomi had a kinsman on her husband's side, a prominent rich man, of the family of Elimelech, whose name was Boaz' (2.1). He behaves like a cricket captain who determines the inclusion and the manner of participation of the players—his servants, the next-of-kin and, in both theory and practice for a while, Ruth. He does not have to overcome obstacles to make the team and occupy his position of authority, power and influence. The potential threat of the unnamed 'closer of kin' never materializes, and, in fact, it is Boaz who carefully orchestrates the event at the gate of the city in which the 'closer of kin' is led to refuse acquiring Naomi's land and consequently marrying Ruth. This 'closer of kin' knows that his own inheritance is at stake—should we not say his identity is on the line?—and chooses the path of nonacquisition of Naomi's land and her Moabite daughter-in-law.

In cricket the captain is free to advise, ask or even demand that a player adopt a particular stance or style. In the end, however, there is freedom for the batsman (batter) or bowler to use his or her judgment and seize the day. As the foreigner who has been included in Naomi's household, Ruth does just that. While 'playing within the boundary' of Naomi's instructions, she disobeys her and takes the initiative to Boaz. It was a situation of life and death for both Naomi and Ruth. The reader is not made aware of Ruth's feelings (what was going on within her), but it is clear that Naomi was aware of both the great potential for life and a future in the success of Ruth's adventure. Naomi has known bitterness; she knows what death means for her identity and the future of the family name. Famine and death have already characterized her life in Bethlehem and Moab, respectively.

Boaz is portrayed as an honourable man. Indeed, it cannot be said of his words and actions, 'That's not cricket'. He exemplifies the type whose loyalty to Yahweh shows itself in the pursuit of the good of those who are powerless and different, with no background to make a claim upon his (Boaz's) goodness. (Of course, Ruth's kindness to Naomi might be such a claim.) Moreover, Naomi's kinship to him, through her deceased husband Elimelech, constituted such a claim. Boaz, for his part, is not passive but active in pursuing the 'closer of kin'; Boaz does so with the promise to be honourable and faithful. He is secure in his identity as an Israelite. Thus, he could say confidently in the presence of the people and the elders,

> Today you are witnesses that I have acquired all that belonged to Elimelech and all that belonged to Chilion and Mahlon. I have also acquired Ruth the Moabite, the wife of Mahlon, to be my wife, to

maintain the dead man's name on his inheritance, in order that the name of the dead may not be cut off from his kindred and from the gate of his native place; today you are witnesses (4.9-10).

The people present, for their part, declare:

> We are witnesses. May the Lord make the woman who is coming into your house like Rachel and Leah, who together built up the house of Israel. May you produce children in Ephrathah and bestow a name in Bethlehem; and, through the children that the Lord will give you by this young woman, may your house be like the house of Perez, whom Tamar bore to Judah (4.11-12).

Israel's identity is indelibly stamped by the inclusion of the foreigner and the 'sinned against' who become mothers of Israel. At the conclusion of the story, Ruth's foreignness is dropped, as the people celebrate with Naomi the birth of Obed; they simply say, 'for your daughter-in-law who loves you, who is more to you than seven sons, has borne him' (4.15).

## Conclusion

Ruth and Kanhai are aliens in their 'new' land; they do not return to the ancestral land to reassume their erstwhile identities. In their respective 'new' worlds, they choose to enter the 'field of play'—should I say 'fields of play'?—and forge a new identity for themselves, and in the process forge a new identity for those who 'naturally' identify with them. But no less decisive, indeed of even greater consequence, they forge a new identity for their respective peoples who are more than those that the narrow 'natural' confines of ethnic, cultural, religious and class purity would include.

For Kanhai and the Indo-West Indians and, indeed, all West Indians, this happens because they live in the in-betweenness of more than one culture, religion, ethnic group. Those who look on see themselves as being uplifted by the triumph against adversity and incredible odds of these two human beings whose fields of play were different but central to those who had so much to gain or lose. We have turned to Ruth with questions of duality, identity and living in the in-betweenness, wondering whether and how God is at work in the very fabric of such contemporary human experiences. Given the centrality of cricket to the sense of identity, personal and communal, of the peoples of the English-speaking Caribbean, that question of the contemporary 'exiles' in their postcolonial world(s) to Ruth and indeed the whole of the Bible as sacred Scripture is unavoidable.

## BIBLIOGRAPHY

Barker, J.S.
1967        'From Wellington to World Champions', in G. Sobers and J.S. Barker (eds.), *Cricket in the Sun: A History of West Indian Cricket* (London: Arthur Barker): 7-37.
Beckles, Hilary (ed.)
1994        *An Area of Conquest* (Kingston: Ian Randle).
Beckles, Hilary, and Brian Stoddard (eds.)
1995        *Liberation Cricket* (Kingston: Ian Randle).
Birbalsingh, F.
1996        *The Rise of Westindian Cricket* (St. John's, Antigua: Hansib).
1988        'Indo-Caribbean Test Cricketers,' in F. Birbalsingh and C. Shiwcharan, *Indo-Westindian Cricket* (London: Hansib): 13-26.
Brearley, M.
1969        'Foreword', in C.L.R. James, *Beyond a Boundary* (London: Stanley Paul): 9-12.
Guttman, Allen
1978        *From Ritual to Record* (New York: Columbia University Press).
Hamlin, John
1996        *Surely There Is a Future* (Grand Rapids: Eerdmans).
Heath, Roy
1988        *The Shadow Bride* (New York: Persea Books).
Hubbard, Robert L.
1988        *The Book of Ruth* (Grand Rapids: Eerdmans).
James, C.L.R.
1969        *Beyond a Boundary.* (London: Stanley Paul).
1986        'Cricket in West Indian Culture', in C.L.R. James, *Cricket* (London: Allison & Busby): 118-24.
Naipaul, V.S.
1987        *The Enigma of Arrival* (London: Penguin Books, 1987).
Shiwcharan, Clem
1988        'The Tiger of Port Mourant—R.B. Kanhai: Fact and Fantasy in the Making of an Indo-Guyanese Legend', in F. Birbalsingh and C. Shiwcharan (eds.), *Indo-Westindian Cricket* (London: Hansib): 41-77.
Sobers, Garfield
1967        'Barbados', in G. Sobers and J.S. Barker (eds.), *Cricket in the Sun: A History of West Indian Cricket* (London: Arthur Barker): 49-52.
Trible, Phyllis
1978        *God and the Rhetoric of Sexuality* (Philadelphia: Fortress Press).

# INDEXES

## INDEX OF REFERENCES

### OLD TESTAMENT

### NEW TESTAMENT

# INDEX OF AUTHORS